Real food
real fast

Published in 2002 by

Merlin Publishing

16 Upper Pembroke Street, Dublin 2, Ireland

Tel: + 353 1 6764373 Fax: + 353 1 6764368

publishing@merlin.ie

www.merlin-publishing.com

British Library Cataloguing in Publication Data

A catalogue record for this book is available from the British Library

ISBN 1-903582-39-3

5 4 3 2 1

Photography by Joanne Murphy

Cover and Book Design by Slick Fish Design

Food Styling and Design by Laura Farrell

Printed by Edelvives, Spain

Real food real fast

Domini Kemp

MERLIN
PUBLISHING

Big Thanks To:

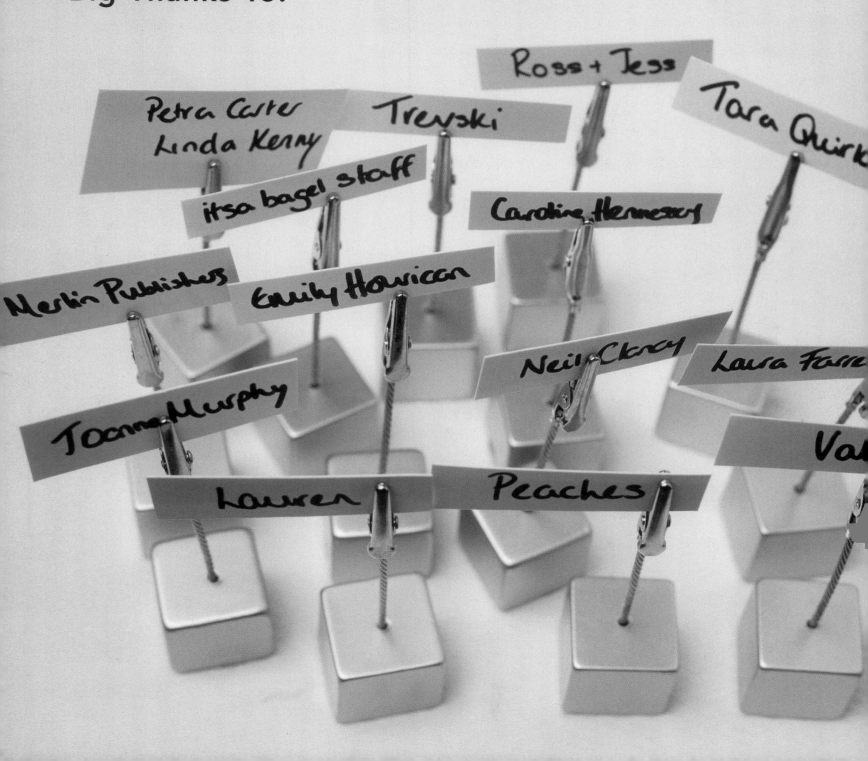

Contents

Rules of Thumb

This book is not a bible by any means. It is not about lecturing people on how and what they should eat. However, it is trying to break down some of the mysteries and culinary confusion that afflict perfectly normal and intelligent people.

It used to confound me that people would religiously follow recipes. Ingredients would be weighed and instructions followed like the Ten Commandments. I could not understand this; it challenged my understanding of people and their relationship with food. I have been cooking for so many years, and it is something I find incredibly easy to do, fun to fix (when hell breaks loose on the stove) and something to enjoy.

Then it all came into focus for me. I love gardens, plants and all things green and outdoorsy. But I can't grow anything. I don't know how to pot plants, prune, take clippings (or is it cuttings?), fertilise, water or weed. It fills me with fear and dread. How do I do this? What equipment do I need? Will I kill this plant also? I want to be green! But how do I do it? This is quite possibly the same situation that many home-cooks find themselves in.

So that food-fear was the motivation for writing this book and collection of recipes. Some of them you have seen before. Others you won't like. But the main point is that the ingredients are widely available, and it is all food you can easily cook at home. If I want to eat lobster, I would like to pay for it in a restaurant. I don't want to be airing out my tiny kitchen for weeks and weeks trying to get rid of the lingering Lobster Thermidor scent. I adore fish, but again like to eat it when I am out. Alternatively I rarely eat pasta when I am out, as I like the stuff made at home a whole lot better.

We all know enough about the perils of food and ingredients. Organic is great, but it is also damned pricey. However in the long run, I think your health and happiness is worth it. Ready-made meals are convenient, but are not as nutritious and satisfying as something home-cooked. We eat so much rubbish nowadays. There is such a hysterical fixation about diet, lifestyle and health – the whole lot has become far too industrial. I like to think that there is something wonderful about having real food for dinner with family and friends.

Here is my list of dos and don'ts. Ignore them if you want! They are guidelines, not gospel.

Store Cupboard Ingredients and Essentials.

Salt and Pepper. *Maldon sea salt* is great, as is the gorgeous grey salt from Guerande, in France. Whichever brand you favour, just try and ensure that it is sea salt you are using. However, for many, salt is salt. It's not. It is singularly the most important component of good food. It is practically religious! Black pepper should always be freshly ground – the coarser the better.

Olive Oil. What can I say? It would be a close contest between salt and olive oil as holy grails of condiments. If I have to skimp on ingredients, the last for a cut back are the salt and olive oil. The pricier the better.

Sugar. I use sugar a lot – even when cooking savoury dishes. Not loads, but enough to bring out flavours especially when cooking onions, or making a rich tomato sauce. If you are adding sugar to something cold (like salad dressing) then use caster sugar. It isn't as crunchy as granulated sugar. If it is going into something hot (like sauces) then granulated is fine to use. Unless it is specified in a recipe here, use any type of sugar you like.

Soy Sauce. I reckon this would be my desert island ingredient along with great olive oil. I have started using the reduced salt soy sauce, but am a fan of *Kikkoman* soy sauce – which I haven't found available in reduced salt variety. Instead, I have a bottle of soy sauce mixed with an equal quantity of water, which I reckon is the same thing.

Worcestershire Sauce. Pretty indispensable stuff since the 1840s. Now a global condiment. Perfect for rich sauces, gravy and marinades.

Balsamic Vinegar. The really good stuff is so rich and soft that it can be served as a digestive in some parts of Italy. I can't imagine doing anything of the sort with the stuff available to us in the supermarkets. This is because the stuff available to us has been made super-fast in factories, and is in no way comparable to the rich brew that takes years and years to age, (hence the big price). Put the genuine stuff on your wish list for guests. They can all chip in and buy you a 200ml (7 fl oz) bottle for the same price as a fancy bottle of champagne!

Honey. A good store cupboard ingredient. I like to add some to gravy and savoury sauces when I want a richer sweetener than just plain old sugar – something sweet, but with body.

Sweet Chilli Sauce. Asian markets are the best place to buy this. Supermarket varieties are just not nice. The really fake looking, bright translucent red sauce, with bits of red floating chilli, is the one to get.

Garlic. Don't need to say anything else. Always have lots of it, and invest in a decent garlic crusher.

Mustard. Plain old Dijon is my favourite. Not a great fan of wholegrain – but it does have its place in life. Just not in my store cupboard!

Ketchup. I have waxed lyrical about the wonders of ketchup throughout the book. It is suffice to say that Heinz is the best variety, and it is also available in organic. How good is that?

Tinned Tomatoes and Passata. Absolutely essential. Italian varieties are gorgeous, but not vital.

Fridge and Freezer Essentials

Buffalo Mozzarella and Parmesan. I love buffalo mozzarella – it's low in fat and fabulous to cook with. Parmesan is equally great – but should be used to enhance flavours giving a sharp little dairy edge, that can elevate something to a greater height. It also seems to never go mouldy – another big plus.

Greek Yoghurt or Crème Fraiche. Both are good to cook with (although crème fraiche is hardier) as alternatives to cream. Natural yoghurt can be too sharp and too unstable to replace cream in sauces, but it can be done. Just don't add yoghurt too early on to a dish. It should go in at the last minute.

Butter. We love butter. Delicious pale unsalted French varieties or the hardy daffodil colour of the salty Irish stuff. It is all equally wonderful – although naturally, I am biased towards the Irish stuff! I hate pseudo healthy low fat spreads. Use real butter (just less of it) if you are worried about consuming too much fat. I tend to use a lot of olive oil when cooking; butter is a treat – but an irreplaceable one. There just isn't a good substitute.

Fresh herbs. Basil, thyme, rosemary, coriander and flatleaf parsley are my indispensable herbs, but sage and tarragon are good too.

Other Rules

- All recipes serve 4 unless otherwise specified.

- Food hygiene is so important. Food poisoning is inconvenient at best, fatal at worst. New legislation is clamping down on food retailers, restaurants, employers and employees within the catering industry and it is serious stuff, with far-reaching implications, many of which are unwelcome within the industry. All decent caterers are very much pro-food legislation that will clamp down on the dirty, filthy creatures that sell to unwitting customers. But, we are not in favour of the kind of broad-brush legislation that will ultimately stop the small manufacturers and cottage industries from operating. They simply cannot produce the same product (especially in the cheese making area) unless the old ways are maintained. It would be a terrible shame to put these vitally important industries out of business because some bright spark in a fast food restaurant decides to defrost turkeys in the cisterns of the staff toilets...

- At home, you must be careful. I have tried to remind you, where possible, that you need to wash your hands after handling raw chicken and meat or fish. I find the safest thing to do, is use a small chopping board (one of the plastic ones), which you should reserve for chopping raw meat on, only. They are usually small enough to fit into your sink and can be easily washed. I like to save my wooden board for vegetables, fruit and bread etc. Just no raw meat or fish. The plastic boards should be washed in cold water first, then scrubbed in hot soapy water and regularly soaked overnight in water to which you've added a small but appropriate amount of bleach. Be sure to treat knives and anything else you have handled with the same care.

- Be sensible about storing food in the refrigerator. Obviously it would be unwise to store some chicken breasts that were leaking above your uncovered aioli. You could have raw chicken juices potentially dripping into a sauce made of uncooked eggs. Not good. Raw meats are stored on the bottom areas of fridges for this reason.

- Food should be covered. Do not put half-used tins in the fridge. Empty your half tin of baked beans into a bowl and cover!

- Don't put piping hot things in the fridge to cool down. If you are making, say, the lasagne or chicken, leek and blue cheese pie, then you must let them cool down at room temperature, then cover and keep in the fridge until ready to cook.

Pasta Pointers

- 100g pasta feeds 1 person.

- Generally try and cook pasta in plenty of boiling water – the ratio should be about 4 times water to pasta.

- Before filling the saucepan with water, I pour a tablespoon of olive oil into the pan and rub it all over the base. Then I fill it up with water and bring it to the boil. I find that this prevents pasta from sticking to the bottom of the pan (which inevitably happens at home).

- Pasta should be cooked at a rolling boil. Avoid any simmering action – save that for your pasta sauce.

- There are many arguments as to whether or not water should be salted before cooking pasta; some say it makes the pasta go hard – others say this is nonsense. Personally I don't bother. I cook the pasta until al dente and check if it's cooked by tasting a little bit. There are other ways of testing it; these include hurling strands of spaghetti against a wall to see whether or not it will stick. If it sticks, it's cooked! But it is easier and less dangerous to simply taste a bit.

- Then, (and this is the sacrilegious bit), I drain and rinse the pasta well with cold water – if I can't use it for a while. If I am using it straight away, I rinse it by pouring a kettle full of boiling water onto it. I think this helps get rid of the starchy stuff that makes pasta stick and congeal, especially if you are a bit inexperienced in the kitchen. Then I pour a good tablespoon of olive oil over the pasta, and toss it (whilst still in the colander, in the sink). Most of the excess water and oil will come off. I also season the pasta very lightly, and sometimes chuck in a clove of crushed garlic. You can put the drained pasta back in the saucepan for a final blast of heat, then dole out onto plates and spoon some sauce on top.

- Always think of pasta as a blank canvas. It is totally and utterly tasteless – so your sauce should always be on the cusp of overpowering. Once you have combined sauce and pasta, any extreme sense of flavour will balance out.

- Dried pasta, (especially Italian varieties) such as the excellent *De Cecco* brand are perfectly acceptable, and in my opinion superior to many of the commercial "fresh" varieties. In this case, fresh isn't the best.

Breakfast, Brunch, Hangover

Eggs Benedict with Sautéed Spinach and Asparagus

The key to successful eggs benedict is organisation and a good Hollandaise. Everyone panics about making this particular sauce, but there is no need. If you screw it up, you can potentially fix it. If not, chuck it out and start again. This luxury wouldn't be allowed in a restaurant kitchen, where the consequences of botching up a large batch of Hollandaise are missing limbs and being made to feel like the kitchen idiot.

Get the Hollandaise made first and out of the way.

4 egg yolks
200g (7oz) butter
squeeze of lemon juice
salt

Put the egg yolks and about a knob of butter in a bowl, set over a saucepan of gently simmering water. This is called a Bain Marie. Make sure the water is not touching the base of the bowl (as this direct contact with the base of the bowl will cause the egg to get too hot, and then scramble). Add a pinch of salt and stir with a wooden spoon – not frantically – but continuously and gently. Gradually the butter should melt, and the sauce should start to feel thicker. It's won't suddenly feel all gloopy and thick like mayonnaise, but there should be a subtle difference in consistency.

Once you have reached this stage, add the lemon juice, and gradually add chunks of the butter. Take your time. Allow a bit to dissolve and to become incorporated before adding more. Keep monitoring the heat. The water should be gently simmering. This whole process should take about 10 minutes, 15 if you are a bit tentative.

Keep going by chucking the butter into the sauce at regular intervals, and constantly but gently stirring. Taste and see if salt or more lemon juice is needed (many people make Hollandaise with unsalted butter, and therefore need to add more seasoning). Your sauce should be as thick as yoghurt! Take off the heat, allow to cool slightly and then cover with cling film and set aside until ready to serve. You can simply put the bowl over some simmering water for a few minutes before serving for a final quick blast of heat.

Remaining ingredients

4 eggs
2 tablespoons white wine vinegar
1-2 bunches asparagus, trimmed
100g (4oz) butter
2 English muffins, sliced in half
500g (1lb) spinach
salt and pepper

Get a frying pan, and fill with water. Bring it up to the boil and add the white wine vinegar. Have a bowl filled with cold water ready to put the eggs into once they are poached.

I have found the easiest way for fool-proof poached eggs is to do it one at a time. Crack an egg into a small ramekin. This is just handy, as you are not fumbling around trying to crack an egg and gently pour it (from a low height) into hot steaming water. The ramekin (or small bowl) means that you can just slip it in with no fuss. Using a slotted spoon, start swirling the water in the frying pan to create a whirlpool effect – think of creating a mini tornado. While the water is swirling, pour the egg in from the ramekin. The stringy bits of egg all wrap around each other, and eventually settle. Keep the water simmering very gently, and after about 1½ minutes, lift the egg out of the saucepan, and straight into the bowl of cold water.

Repeat the process with the other three eggs. It is really important not to have the water in the frying pan boiling vigorously, as you will just end up making egg soup!

Cook the asparagus in a saucepan of boiling water, for about 2 minutes. Drain and rinse in cold water, then set aside.

Go and relax for ten minutes or half an hour. The next stage will take about 10-15 minutes and needs to be done in one go, and then served immediately!

Toast or warm the muffins in a low oven. Boil the kettle. Warm up 4 plates in the oven. Add some boiling water to the Bain Marie (this will give the Hollandaise a final blast of safe heat) and place the bowl of Hollandaise on top. Remove the cling film and give it a little stir as it gently warms up. Drain most of the cold water out of the poached eggs, and top up with boiling water. Have some paper towel ready to pat the eggs dry just before they go on the plate.

Heat some butter in a large saucepan or frying pan. Add most of the spinach and a good sprinkle of salt and pepper. Keep the heat up high, and quickly cook until the spinach has wilted. At the same time, heat up the remaining butter in a medium frying pan, and fry the asparagus for a minute. Season well and turn off the heat. Get your 4 plates out, and place a muffin in the centre of each one. Take a good spoonful of spinach, squeezing out excess liquid against the side of the saucepan and place equal amounts onto the four muffins. Top with a poached egg. Spoon over lashings of Hollandaise and serve with the sautéed asparagus.

Breakfast Sandwiches

These are a decadent type of sandwich – not over stuffed, but fried in butter so that the filling melts. The best fillings are your favourite cheeses, roast or cured meats and fresh herbs. Use white or brown bread, whichever you prefer, but let it go a bit stale before frying – otherwise it ends up absorbing too much butter (damned shame). One of my favourite combinations is buffalo mozzarella, pesto, bresaola and fresh spinach... or roasted red peppers with sliced artichoke hearts, Parma ham and Parmesan with generous drizzles of olive oil....

8 pieces buttered bread
4 tomatoes sliced
salt and pepper
2 tablespoons Dijon mustard
1 teaspoon honey
4 slices smoked mozzarella
4 slices cheddar
4 slices roast ham
few pieces basil
olive oil
butter

When you have buttered the bread, make 4 piles of two, sticking the buttered sides together so they don't stick to anything else. Season the tomatoes with some salt and pepper. Mix together the Dijon and honey, and then spread on one side of the bread. Top with tomatoes, the cheeses, ham and basil. Drizzle with a little olive oil, and top with the other piece of buttered bread. The buttered sides should be on the outside of the sandwich.

Heat up a generous knob of butter in a large frying pan. Press two sandwiches onto the surface, gently fry until golden brown and then flip over and cook the other side. Remove from the pan, repeat with the other two sandwiches, slice in half and serve with extra honey-Dijon mixture. The cheeses can get very hot, so be careful if you are handing these out to kids.

Crème Fraiche Brulée with Sugar Roasted Fruits

I have only once tried to make crème brulée at home. The results were pretty disgusting – it became crème scrambled eggs very quickly. My grill just doesn't get nearly hot enough. So I am not going to lie and tell you that your "brulée" will look like the photo. It won't. But you can get a blow torch (available for about €20-40($30)), which will help you attain that "restaurant look". The "brulée" part of this dessert is sheer laziness.

You can use any available fruits – I like figs, peaches, apricots – but these aren't always available, and when out of season and imported from Timbuktu, they are really very tasteless. You can substitute apples, pears and bananas or anything that's readily available. You can also garnish the fruits with some chopped mint or chopped pistachio nuts.

450g (1lb) crème fraiche
2 peaches
4 apricots
4 figs
250g (9oz) sugar
2 tablespoons honey

Divide the crème fraiche in to 4-6 ramekins, cover with cling film and freeze overnight.

Preheat your grill to its highest setting. Slice the fruits in half, remove any stones, and place on a roasting tray. Sprinkle half the sugar directly onto the fruits, and grill for up to 15 minutes (keep an eye on them) until they are caramelised looking. Set aside. Sprinkle the remaining sugar on top of the crème fraiche, and then attack with the blow torch until the top is all caramelised and looks like the photo! Serve the ramekins on a plate with the roasted fruits.

If your attempts to make the brulée fail, simply mix the crème fraiche or similar amount of Greek yoghurt with two tablespoons of honey and serve with the roasted fruits.

Lemon and Poppyseed Loaf with Banana and Coconut Butter

This easy loaf also works particularly well if served warm with some butter and a little honey or a sprinkling of icing sugar. The banana butter is delicious served with everything from scones to yoghurt, and very popular with kids.

Lemon and Poppyseed Loaf

greaseproof paper
(the one that says "no fat needed")
2 eggs
110g (4oz) butter
170g (6oz) sugar
170g (6oz) self raising flour
4 tablespoons milk
grated juice and zest of 1 lemon
1 tablespoon poppy seeds

Preheat oven to 180ºC (350ºF).

Line a loaf tin (900g (2lb) tin) with greaseproof paper; you might need to use a little butter to make the paper stick to the sides of the tin. In a medium sized bowl, beat the eggs and then add all the remaining ingredients. Use an electric mixer to blend everything together.

Pour the mixture into the loaf tin, and smooth the top of the cake. Bake for about 45 minutes. The cake should be a lovely golden colour and firm to the touch. When the cake has cooled slightly, remove from the tin. Slice and serve with the banana and coconut butter.

Banana and Coconut Butter

50g (2oz) butter
2 tablespoons caster sugar
4 bananas, roughly chopped
1 vanilla bean or ½ teaspoon
vanilla essence
juice of 1 lemon
100ml (4 fl oz) coconut milk

Melt the butter in a medium sized saucepan. Add the sugar and gently heat until it starts to melt. Add the bananas and turn up the heat. When the bananas start to caramelise, scrape in the vanilla seeds from the pod (or add the vanilla essence), and add the lemon juice and coconut milk. Boil until the milk has reduced and the mixture is quite thick. Remove from the heat, and purée if necessary. I personally like to leave it chunkier. This butter can be served warm or chilled.

Potato Cakes with Capers and Smoked Salmon

These are deliciously savoury and salty, and work best washed down with a Bloody Mary. All the breakfast favourites in one tasty dish. Serve with a big dollop of sour cream to which you've added some finely chopped chives, or if you are really trying to spoil someone, a little spoonful of caviar!

500g (1lb) potatoes
50g (2oz) butter
2 red onions, peeled and finely chopped
1 teaspoon caster sugar
salt and black pepper
1 tablespoons capers, drained and rinsed
small bunch dill, finely chopped
small bunch parsley, finely chopped
squeeze lemon juice
1 egg, beaten
60g (2oz) white flour
50ml (4 tablespoons) olive oil (approx.)
4 – 8 slices smoked salmon
4 tablespoons sour cream mixed with some chopped chives
extra slices of red onions, lemon wedges and capers to garnish

Peel the potatoes, and boil for about 10-15 minutes until tender. Drain and mash. You can do this up to 48 hours in advance. Melt the butter and fry the onions for a couple of minutes, then add the sugar and season with plenty of pepper – but go easy on the salt as the capers are very salty. In a bowl, mix together the cold potatoes, fried onions, capers, herbs, lemon juice and egg. Shape into 4 large patties. If the mixture is too dry, add a little melted butter or sour cream. Dust with flour.

Heat the oil in a large frying pan. Fry the cakes over a medium heat on both sides until golden brown. Transfer to a roasting tray or gratin dish and cover with tin foil. The potato cakes will be fine in the oven for up to 30 minutes at 150°C (300°F).

If you want to precook these, fry them off, and transfer to a roasting tray and set aside – leave them to cool, then cover and keep in the fridge overnight. When ready to serve, uncover and heat for about 15 minutes in a moderate oven at 180°C (350°F). Serve with slices of smoked salmon and other garnishes.

Open Club Sambos

Club sandwiches are the staple of so many hotel room-service menus. That special something you yearn for after a long journey, best accompanied by some skinny, crispy chips and loads of ketchup. Bliss. Except that, more often than not, they can disappoint. That's why you should make your own – just get someone to wait on you for that in-house, room-service experience. Serve these on any type of bread – but if you use thick slices, use only 2 slices per person. Using a whole chicken breast per sandwich may sound a bit too much – but sometimes the breasts are tiny, and you may be starving.

3-4 chicken breasts, skin removed
1-2 tablespoons olive oil
50g (2oz) butter
salt and freshly ground black pepper
8-12 slices bacon
2 avocadoes
juice of 1 lemon
8-12 pieces of bread
4 tomatoes, sliced
4 tablespoons mayonnaise
2 handfuls lettuce

Slice the chicken into thin slices. Be sure to wash this board and your hands very carefully before handling any other food or utensils. Heat the olive oil in a large frying pan. When the oil is hot, fry the chicken slices for a couple of minutes on both sides. If you are unsure as to when you should flip the slices, only do so when you can! If they are not ready, they will stick to the pan, and will only release themselves when they are ready to be turned over. Season the chicken well and add the butter. Cook over a medium heat until the slices are fully cooked. Transfer to a gratin dish and cover with tin foil.

Meanwhile grill the bacon on both sides until it is very crispy and you've cooked off most of the fat. When it is cooked, transfer to a plate with kitchen paper, and pat off excess fat. Cut the avocadoes in half, remove the stone and scoop out the flesh. Season and add the lemon juice. Mash with a fork, and set aside.

Grill the bread in the oven, or simply toast it. Butter one side, and spread some mashed avocado on the other side. Add the sliced tomatoes and slices of bacon. Top with lettuce, a layer of chicken and spread with mayonnaise. Close the sandwiches and serve.

Bloody Mary

We take no prisoners here, this is absolutely not for the faint-hearted. Too many bartenders serve tasteless glasses of insipid red juice, which do nothing to alleviate the symptoms of a genuine hangover sufferer. In a restaurant in London I was once offered a Bloody Mary, which was to be made with fresh tomatoes. I thought this would be a wonderful idea, and was delighted at the suggestion. Twenty minutes later, a pale and truly revolting pinky-red foul juice arrived. It might be a lovely idea, if made from the most delicious vine ripened tomatoes, but with regular old supermarket tomatoes, it ain't going to work. Bottled tomato juice tastes good, simply because there is so much salt in it – it's like ketchup – the homemade stuff just isn't as appealing. Speaking of which, I do put a dash of ketchup into these drinks. Don't squirm or balk at this idea. Just do it, and if you don't like it, leave it out next time – same goes for the horseradish sauce – which needs to be a pretty good variety. If it's a really cheap n' cheerful brand, use less. Make the Bloody Marys a few hours in advance and chill. I don't like to serve these with too much ice, as it goes all watery and anaemic, like the aforementioned torture-drink. As it is almost a meal in itself, serve it with something light and tasty, like the fried sandwiches. A big plate of eggs Benedict might all be a bit too much for Saturday night sinners....

1 litre (1¾ pints) tomato juice
200ml (⅓ pint) vodka
4 tablespoons Worcestershire sauce
2 tablespoons horseradish sauce
1 tablespoon ketchup
juice of 3 lemons
1 tablespoon Tabasco sauce
black pepper
good sprinkling celery salt
4 sticks celery, washed and trimmed
1 lemon or lime, cut into wedges, for decoration

In a jug or bowl, whisk all the ingredients (except for the celery sticks and lemon/lime wedges!) with half the tomato juice. When everything has blended well, add the remaining tomato juice and chill.

Serve in glasses with a small bit of ice, lemon or lime wedges and sticks of celery.

Goddess Juice

Without a doubt, juicers are the kitchen appliance for the caring, sharing and nutritionally challenged. All that goodness in one delicious sup. A liquid guarantee, generously providing a clean slate; a new beginning. The beetroot and orange combinations are kind of hard to do after a night on the town. This one fits the bill, refreshing and zingy enough to revive many a comatose creature.

8 Granny Smith apples
2 pears
1 pineapple
2cm (1 inch) piece of ginger
bunch parsley

Leave the skin on the apples and pears, wash them well and chop into chunks. Discard the cores. Cut the skin off the pineapple, and cut into chunks small enough to fit into your juicer. Remove the skin from the ginger, juice all of the ingredients, and then pass through a sieve. If any foam rises to the surface of the juice, remove with a metal spoon and discard. Refrigerate until ready to serve.

P.S. Fresh squeezed juices are a great way to pack loads of vitamins and nutrients into kids that are picky about what they scoff. I am absolutely horrified at the amount of fluorescent drinks resembling anti-freeze, directly marketed to children and falsely posing as 'good for you'. Rubbish! Have you ever read the ingredients on some of those concoctions? I would rather clean a car engine with them, than give them to humans. I am able to pack a few organic apples, oranges and carrots into my little monster every morning without fuss - which I am convinced keeps her happy, healthy and the colds at bay. Bananas work well, and tend to bulk up a juice making it more of a meal, as does mixing lots of berries with yoghurt and making smoothies in a blender. Parsley and basil are delicious to throw in to the mix, and will always perk up the colour.

Afternoon Delights

Afternoon Delights

Pistachio and Chocolate Biscuits

My cousin Tara (recipe tester extraordinaire) called these biscuits "the work of Satan". She is normally a pretty strict, no-wheat kind of gal, but for these gooey, chocolaty devils, she happily fell off the coeliac wagon.

It helps to have a couple of baking sheets in order to do this recipe, but if not, it doesn't matter. Just have sheets of baking paper that fit the baking tray ready. If the paper won't stick to the tray, use a little blob of the biscuit mixture to hold it down.

Makes about 14 biscuits

75g (3oz) butter
250g (9oz) dark chocolate
3 tablespoons cream
150g (5oz) pistachio nuts
100g (4oz) caster sugar
100g (4oz) plain flour

Preheat oven to 180°C (350°F).

Melt the butter, chocolate and cream together in a heatproof bowl over a saucepan of gently simmering water or else in the microwave, covered in cling film. In a food processor, blend the nuts with the sugar and flour until they become very fine in texture. Gradually add the chocolate mixture and continue to process until it resembles a soft dough.

Take a tablespoon-full of the mixture and place on the baking tray. Lightly pat down, and repeat with the remaining mixture. You will probably only be able to fit about 6 biscuits on the baking tray. Bake for about 7 minutes, and then remove from the oven, and transfer the biscuits onto a wire rack to cool. Continue to cook the remaining biscuits and once they are cool store in an airtight container until ready to serve. You can reheat them, and get them all gooey by giving them a 3-5 second blast in the microwave.

Crunchy Banana Muffins

Make sure you inform people that these contain nuts before doling out at brunch. I once nearly killed a Sunday guest by failing to do so, but they got us back by trying to sneak some prawns into my sister's pasta one night (she's highly allergic to shellfish)... Anyway, all was forgiven, but I'm never inviting those lunatics round to my house again...

Makes about 20 muffins. You will need a muffin tray (or two) and muffin papers.

450g (1lb) flour
450g (1lb) sugar
2 teaspoons baking powder
1 teaspoon bicarbonate of soda
½ teaspoon salt
225g (8oz) butter, melted but not boiling hot
2 eggs
180ml (⅓ pint) milk
1 teaspoon vanilla extract
100g (4oz) raisins and/or sultanas
100g (4oz) dried banana chips, roughly chopped
100g (4oz) granola cereal
100g (4oz) chopped walnuts

Preheat oven to 180°C (350°F).

Line your muffin tray with muffin papers. In a bowl mix the flour, sugar, baking powder, bicarbonate of soda and salt. Mix the butter with the milk, eggs and vanilla extract in a cake mixer or food processor or with a whisk. Fold the dry mixture into the liquid, or mix it all up in the cake mixer or food processor. Fold in the raisins, banana chips, granola and walnuts.

When the mix is well blended, spoon about one or two dessertspoons into each muffin case. The muffin mixture should reach the same level as the tray. Bake for about 20 minutes. Remove from the oven and repeat with any remaining mixture. Cool the muffins on a wire rack and keep in an airtight container or wrap individually in cling film.

Tried; Tested and We Work Brownies

These have been cooked countless numbers of times. They really do work, and are the end result of many tweaks and changes to a multitude of brownie recipes. When they have cooked, the top will look a bit anaemic and unappetising – but don't worry. Didn't your mother always tell you not to judge a book by its cover? Well, the same applies here. They might look like you have used that revolting fake chocolate, but underneath lies some good chocolatey, gooey, fudgey brownie. You can always pour over some extra melted choclate, for that special splurge.

You need an electric beater, cake mixer, or strong biceps to whisk up this mix.

Makes 9 generous brownies.

180g (6oz) butter
150g (5oz) dark good quality chocolate
3 eggs
250g (8oz) caster sugar
1 teaspoon vanilla essence
110g (4oz) plain flour, sieved
1 teaspoon baking powder

Preheat oven to 170°C (325°F).

Melt the butter and chocolate together in a bowl over gently simmering water.

Whisk the eggs, caster sugar and vanilla essence together until pale and thick. Divide this mixture into two separate bowls. Leave one of the bowls alone, but whisk the second bowl a bit more – until it has doubled in volume. Add the melted chocolate to the first bowl of whisked egg and sugar. Then fold the second bowl of whisked egg and sugar into the chocolate and egg mixture.

Fold in the flour and baking powder, spread into a rectangular cake tin (approximately 28 x 20cm (12 x 7 inches)) and bake for about 25 minutes. The brownies will be quite gooey in the middle. Allow them to cool fully, and then cut into squares. If you wrap the brownies in cling film, they will keep for two days.

Pear and Apple Crumble

Once you've made this a few times, you can substitute and play around with different fruit combinations. Add any favourite spices, such as cinnamon, vanilla or star anise – although personally I like to leave it fairly plain. You can always make the crumble topping, even if you don't have the recipe. Just remember "half fat to flour, and a quarter sugar"; (if you use 500g (1lb) flour, you will use 250g (8oz) butter and 125g (4oz) sugar). Easy as crumble!

300g (12oz) flour
150g (6oz) butter
175g (7oz) sugar
5 cooking apples, peeled, cored and sliced
5 pears, peeled, cored and sliced

Preheat oven to 180ºC (350ºF).

In a food processor, mix the flour, butter and 75g (3oz) sugar. Process until the mixture resembles crumbs. You can do this by hand – mix the flour and sugar together, and cut the butter into small pieces. Using your hands, rub the flour and butter lightly together to eventually create a crumb-like mixture. You can do this 24 hours in advance. Just chill and leave to rest overnight.

Grease a gratin dish about 20 x 30cm (7 x 12 inches) with a little butter, and layer up the apples and pears with sprinkles of the remaining 100g (4oz) sugar. Top with the crumble mixture and bake for about 35-40 minutes, or until the crumble topping is golden brown. Serve with ice cream or sweetened Greek yoghurt.

Ricotta and Cookie Crumble

This is really a dessert for kids, especially popular in the summer and autumn months, served with berries and ice cream. Once they've had a bite, grown-ups regularly tuck into it on the sly, even after scoffing about the lack of sophistication... snobs.

Make this in a small sandwich tin or cake tin.

175g (6oz) Oreo cookies
200g (7oz) dark chocolate
150g (5oz) white chocolate
250g (9oz) ricotta cheese

Preheat oven to 160°C (310°F).

Crush up the Oreo cookies whatever way you like. Helpful hint: kids will love you forever if you let them do their own culinary interpretation of this nifty move. Crumble them in your hands. Squash them in their packets, if individually wrapped. Whatever!

Break the chocolate into small bite-sized pieces. Mix the whole lot together as best you can. Spread into the tin and bake for about 25 minutes until the chocolate is all melted and gooey. Allow to cool slightly, then serve with some ice cream or yoghurt. If you don't want to use Oreo cookies, you could also try this home made chocolate chip cookie dough crumb.

Mix together in a food processor: 100g (4oz) flour, 50g (2oz) sugar, 25g (1oz) sugar, 50g (2oz) dark chocolate, broken into pieces. Pack half this mixture into the bottom of the tin, mix the chocolate and ricotta together, spread that in the middle, and top with the remaining crumb mixture. Bake for maybe 30 minutes at the same temperature. Allow to cool slightly and then serve.

Mincemeat Flapjacks

It's true, mince pies used to be made with minced beef – tongue or brisket, or sometimes even venison – flavoured with cinnamon and allspice. In ye olden days, the sugar and alcohol helped preserve the meat – it is only quite recently that the meat was replaced with more fruit and suet. After all the Christmas turkey, booze and bread sauce, a mince pie with a nice cup of tea is a welcome respite! But more often than not, the pastry is pretty revolting. That is why I like these guys. Good quality mince is easy to buy or you could make your own as it's not too difficult. I will leave you with a rough recipe for the filling.

Makes about 12-15 very generous flapjacks. Use a large roasting tin; a 37.5 x 25.75 x 2cm (15 x 8 x 1 inch) baking tray will make them easier to slice, but you might have a bit too much filling for this size.

Recipe for dedicated cooks for mincemeat filling (not obligatory!)

2 Granny Smith apples
150g (5oz) sultanas
150g (5oz) raisins
150g (5oz) currants
100g (3oz) chopped mixed peel
100g (3oz) shredded suet
zest and juice of 1 lemon and1 orange
1 teaspoon mixed spice
150g (4oz) soft brown sugar
4 tablespoons brandy

Flapjacks
450g (1lb) butter
1kg (2lb, 4oz) rolled oats
800g (1lb, 12oz) mincemeat or
recipe above

Peel, core and dice the apples. Mix all the ingredients together and leave to soak (macerate) for a few hours or overnight if possible. This could easily be made a few days in advance and left covered in the fridge.

Preheat oven to 150°C (300°F).
Melt the butter and mix with the oats. Pack half of the oat mixture onto the bottom of the tray or tin, spread over the mince mixture, and then top with the remaining oats. Spread the oats as evenly as you can, with a spatula or your hands. Then bake for 25-30 minutes, until the top is golden brown. Allow to cool in the tin before slicing and serving. They are pretty hard to cut into neat squares, so I prefer to serve them up like slices of pie.

Dinner Party

Dinner Party

Seared Tuna with Celeriac and Soy Salad

I personally don't think that tuna works well with most carbohydrates (except in Japanese cooking), such as potatoes, rice or pasta. It is sometimes OK with lentils – but more often than not, I prefer it with light, salad-type garnishes like guacamole and this celeriac salad – which is almost noodle-like. Tuna is destroyed once it is cooked beyond the colour shown in this photo. Sorry, but if you want it well done, open a can of the stuff. Tuna can be very pricey and mediocre – so finding a good fishmonger is important. Avoid tuna that has blood lines or bruising. Remember that 100g (4oz) is good for a starter, 200g (7oz) for a main course (as we have done here).

1 celeriac
juice of 1 lemon
1 tablespoon olive oil
1 tablespoon soy sauce
squeeze of lime juice
salt and black pepper
2 tomatoes, finely diced
1 avocado, peeled and diced
small bunch coriander, finely chopped
400g (14oz) tuna, probably 2 x
200g (7oz) tuna loin steaks
olive oil
50g (2oz)butter

Cut the celeriac in half and then quarter it. Cut off the skin and discard. When you have manageable pieces, cut into very long thin strips (like short spaghetti). Bring a small saucepan of water to boil, and add the lemon juice. Have a colander ready in the sink. Blanch the celeriac in small batches in the boiling water for about 1 minute. Transfer the celeriac "spaghetti" to the colander using a slotted spoon, and rinse under cold running water. Continue until all the celeriac is blanched and refreshed. When it has drained, pat dry with paper towel. Place the celeriac in a bowl with the olive oil, soy sauce and lime juice. Taste and season. You could also drizzle a little sesame oil or add toasted sesame seeds into the mixture. Mix with the tomato, avocado and coriander and set aside while you sear off the tuna.

Heat a teaspoon of olive oil per steak until the oil is smoking. Season the tuna super-generously, especially with the black pepper, and cook for 15 seconds on each sides. It'll take this long, providing your pan is hot enough. Lay the fish in the pan, and count: "one Mississippi, two Mississippi" etc. until you get to 15, then chuck in a generous knob of butter, flip the steak over and repeat the Mississippi chanting.

Transfer to a clean plate and repeat with the other steak. Leave the tuna to rest for at least five minutes and then cut into 1-2cm (½–1 inch) thick slices. Serve with the celeriac salad, or even some guacamole (see page 47).

Onion Tarte Tatin with Goat's Cheese Cream

Traditionally, Tarte Tatin is the famous upside down tart created by the Tatin sisters at the beginning of the century. I absolutely adore it as a dessert, served with spanking fresh vanilla ice cream oozing onto the unctuous caramel and buttery pastry layers. This tarte is savoury, and I have added a little rice flour to the pastry, which makes the texture a lot more interesting. Think shortcrust pastry with a hint of crushed Digestive biscuits.... A big blob of goat's cheese cream makes this a wonderful starter. Use white or red onions – doesn't matter – whichever you prefer. You will need a large ovenproof frying pan for this recipe to work really well. If you can't find one, use a roasting tin. It'll look a lot more rustic, but who cares! Make the pastry the night before or even days before, and then freeze. Either way, do it first. Serves 6-8 as a starter, 4-6 as a main course.

Pastry
170g (6oz) white flour
50g (2oz) ground rice
120g (4oz) butter
2 teaspoons cold water

Mix all the ingredients together in the food processor. If the pastry doesn't fully come together to form one lump of dough, add a bit more water. Wrap in cling film and refrigerate until you are ready to roll it out. Give the food processor a quick wash, and while you have it out, make the goat's cheese cream.

Cream
250g (9oz) goat's cheese
100ml (4fl oz) cream
2 tablespoons chopped fresh herbs: parsley, basil, chervil

Blend all the ingredients together, season with black pepper and chill until ready to use.

Filling
50g (2oz) butter
1kg (2lb) onions, peeled and finely sliced
3 cloves garlic, peeled and crushed
salt and freshly ground black pepper
1 teaspoon sugar
50g (2oz) raisins
rosemary or other herbs, finely chopped

Preheat oven to 200°C (400°F). Melt the butter in a large ovenproof frying pan or saucepan and sweat the onions until soft. Add the garlic, season lightly, then add the sugar, raisins and herbs. Turn up the heat and allow the onions to caramelise. Taste and set aside. Roll out the pastry to fit the size of the frying pan (or failing that, the roasting tin). Cover the onion mixture with the pastry "carpet" and place in the oven. Bake for about ½ an hour – or until the pastry is a nice golden brown. Take out of the oven, and leave for ten minutes before inverting onto a plate. Slice and serve with a spoonful of the goat's cheese cream.

Balsamic Mushrooms with Broccoli and Garlic

This is just a really nice simple starter, ideal for vegetarians, or as a precursor to something quite rich. You can layer up the mushroom with garden lettuce and serve it up with an omelette for a handy supper dish. You need to make the balsamic and soy sauce dip for this (see page 64), but that's a pretty speedy affair. Broccoli rabe works better in this recipe – its delicate leaves and florets seem to easily absorb these kind of flavours, but it can be difficult to get.

4 large field mushrooms
1 quantity of balsamic and soy sauce dip (see page 64)
1 tablespoon olive oil
1 head broccoli, or about 8 stalks of broccoli rabe
4 cloves garlic, peeled and crushed
salt and black pepper
extra olive oil
few Parmesan shavings

Preheat your grill to its highest setting.

Peel the skin of the mushrooms from the underneath up towards the top. Remove the stalk by gently, but firmly, pulling it off. Place the mushrooms in a roasting tin and pour a good tablespoon of the balsamic and soy sauce dip over each mushroom. Grill on the top shelf for about 7-10 minutes.

While these are grilling, heat up the olive oil in a large frying pan. When the oil is hot, add the broccoli and garlic. Season well and fry over a high heat until the broccoli is starting to burn slightly. This gives the dish a wonderful taste. Plate up the mushrooms and top with the fried broccoli. Drizzle with extra olive oil, if you like, and some Parmesan shavings.

Gratin Potatoes

I never fail to get loads of compliments for this version of *Pommes Dauphinoise.* The secret is simple. I cook the potato and cream mixture in a large saucepan for about ten minutes before transferring to a gratin dish. This really helps ensure accurate seasoning, as you can taste the seasoned mixture before it goes in the oven, as opposed to endlessly layering up spuds, cream, salt and pepper, but not really knowing what it tastes like.

Traditionally, *Pommes Dauphinoise.* is made by rubbing a gratin dish with some butter and a clove of garlic, followed by layers of spuds, cream, salt and perhaps a little nutmeg. I prefer to do mine with less cream (milk instead), more garlic and a good topping of cheese that goes all brown and crispy. This cheesy topping is always a prime target for guests.

Knob butter
1kg (2lb) potatoes (all purpose, large)
washed and thinly sliced
(leave the skins on)
300ml (½ pint) cream
300ml (½ pint) milk
salt and pepper
2-3 cloves garlic, peeled and crushed
200g (7oz) grated cheese (Swiss and
Mozzarella are good)

Preheat oven to 180ºC (350ºF).

Rub the gratin dish with butter. Put the sliced potatoes, cream, milk and garlic in a large saucepan and gently bring to the boil. There should be enough liquid to generously cover the potatoes. If not, top up by adding equal quantities of milk and cream. Cook the potatoes by gently simmering the mixture for about 5-10 minutes. Taste the liquid, and make sure it's salty enough. Remove from the heat, scoop out the spuds and layer them fairly neatly in a gratin dish. Pour in the creamy liquid. Again, make sure there is enough to just cover the spuds. Top with grated cheese and bake for about 30 minutes. Remove the foil and bake for a further 15-20 minutes. Stick a knife into the centre to check that the potatoes are very soft – you should not feel anything remotely crunchy! If you do, cook for another 15-20 minutes. Remove from the oven and let the gratin sit for about 5 minutes before serving. Gorgeous with roast chicken, or even on it's own as a supper dish accompanied by salad (add lots of fresh herbs), and our best ever vinaigrette (see page 84).

Chicken Fajitas

It's easy to slag off all those tacky American and Tex-Mex restaurants, with their inevitable quesadillas, burritos and obligatory nachos on the menu. We all flocked to them at one stage, but have come to realise that they don't taste as good as they used to. It makes me sad; when Tex-Mex food is done well, it can be damned good.

A dinner party is the perfect excuse to indulge in something south of the border. Crack open the margaritas, and invite some pals over. This food is always best to eat in large numbers. Three chicken breasts is loads to serve for 4 people, as long as you've got other things such as grated cheese, sour cream, guacamole, salsa and refried beans (YUCK!) going on – but you can certainly up the quantity, if you wish.

Marinade:
50ml (4 tablespoons) olive oil
2 tablespoons ketchup
½ teaspoon smoked paprika
(or American barbecue seasoning –
available in the dried herb section
of supermarkets)
1 tablespoon soy sauce
1 teaspoon sugar
2 cloves garlic, peeled and crushed
salt and black pepper

1 red pepper, deseeded and finely sliced
1 small red onion, peeled and finely sliced
3 chicken breasts, skin removed
lime wedges and flour tortillas, to serve

Mix all the ingredients for the marinade together in a large bowl, and season with salt and plenty of black pepper. After you have sliced the peppers and onions, slice the chicken into long strips. Be sure to wash your hands, chopping board and knife very carefully before handling anything else. Put the pepper, onion and chicken into the marinade and mix well. You can leave this to marinate overnight, in the fridge.

Preheat oven to 180°C (350°F).

Have an ovenproof serving dish ready. Heat up a frying pan until very hot. Add the chicken and shake the pan. Keep the heat up high and allow it to sizzle and cook on all sides. Remember not to force the chicken pieces to flip over if stuck to the pan – when it is good and brown, it will release itself. However, the sugar and ketchup will make it stick more than usual – so if you feel it's burning, you can give it a bit of help to unstick, using an appropriate utensil. Transfer to the serving dish and cook for a further 10 minutes in the oven. At this stage, you can assemble all the other condiments. Wrap up tortillas in tin foil, (sprinkle a few drops of water on to them first), and heat them in the oven on a lower shelf than the chicken for about 5-10 minutes. Serve with lemon wedges, guacamole, salsa, grated cheese and sour cream.

Guacamole

I adore guacamole for its buttery, garlicky, healthy goodness. It does discolour very quickly, but don't let that stop you from making it ahead of time. Once it's ready, spoon it into your serving bowl, smooth over the surface so that it's pretty flat and then squeeze another lime on top so that a layer of lime juice is covering the guacamole. If you don't like guacamole too citrusey, then reduce the quantity of limes down to one.

Avocadoes are often either too ripe or rock solid when you get them in a supermarket. It is such a pleasure when you slice one in half and find glorious green flesh everywhere – not a brown bruise in sight. Buy them two or three days before you need them and err on the harder side. If you leave avocadoes in a brown paper bag at room temperature for a few days, they will soon ripen. Alternatively, if they are a bit too ripe and you need to slow down the ripening process, stick them in the fridge.

2 avocadoes	Cut the avocadoes in half, remove the stone and scoop out the flesh. Mash with a fork, mix with the garlic and lime juice. Season well and cover with a layer of extra lime juice unless you are going to serve straight away.
2 cloves of garlic, peeled and crushed	
juice of 1 or 2 limes (see above)	
salt and black pepper	

Salsa

I love this salsa with everything from fajitas to wraps and even sprinkled over grilled fish. The pricier the tomato, the better – especially when buying vine ripened tomatoes. But, tis worth it for this little recipe.

4 tomatoes, finely diced	Mix all the ingredients together and leave to marinate for 30 minutes before serving.
1 small red onion, peeled and very finely diced	
½ teaspoon caster sugar	
1 small red chilli	
1 teaspoon sweet chilli sauce	
small bunch coriander, finely chopped	
juice of 2 limes	
salt and pepper	

Pan Fried Veal, Parmesan and Sage

Veal is one of those meats that always causes quite a stir – politically rather than culinary-wise – so be warned. Personally, I don't like it rare – it's much nicer served pink. This is because it's a pale meat, and if it's too rare, you start to feel you are consuming undercooked chicken or pork – which is just plain old unpleasant and dangerous. This is beautiful served with the white bean purée (see page 50).

600-800g (1½ – 2lb) loin of veal
50ml (4 tablespoons) olive oil
100g (4oz) butter
small handful of sage, roughly chopped
squeeze of lemon juice
grated Parmesan

Trim any excess fat off the loin, and cut into thick steaks. If you want to prep the meat in advance, at this stage you would wrap them neatly in cling film and keep them stored in the fridge.

Preheat oven to 180°C (350°F).

Bring the meat to room temperature before cooking it (this should take about 15 minutes, provided your kitchen is not like a sauna). Have a roasting tin ready. Heat half the olive oil in a large frying pan. Let it get really hot, on the verge of smoking, and quickly season the veal generously with salt and pepper before adding to the pan. Fry the steaks, two at a time for about three minutes on each side. Leave them alone until you can easily flip them over. Add half the butter and sage. Once the steaks are good and browned on both sides, add a squeeze of lemon juice. Give the saucepan a little shake and transfer the veal and juices to the roasting tin. Repeat with the other two steaks – don't bother washing the saucepan, just add the remaining olive oil and start again. Cover the veal with tin foil and put into the oven for about 10 minutes to cook a little longer.

When ready to serve, put the steaks onto plates, spooning some of the juices and sage on top. Grate a little Parmesan over them – it gives a definite edge you will appreciate. Serve with lemon wedges and a bowl of white bean purée, with lemon parsley and garlic (see page 50).

White Bean Purée with Lemon, Parsley and Garlic

This is dead easy and totally versatile. Leave the purée a little chunky – it goes really well with meat and chicken (as well as hardy types of fish, like cod or haddock). If you over process the purée (which I always do), it will turn out like hummous. It doesn't matter though, as it still tastes great – lumpy or smooth. This is a good recipe to do the night before. It can be reheated at the last minute, although you might need to add a little water and olive oil as the night in the fridge will have dried it out. You can always add stock or some cooked bacon to give it more flavour.

1 tablespoon olive oil
2 x 400g (14oz) tins cannellini beans,
drained and rinsed
3 cloves garlic, peeled and crushed
salt and pepper
juice of 1 lemon
200ml (⅓ pint) water or stock
handful of flatleaf parsley, finely
chopped

Heat up everything except the parsley in a medium-sized saucepan, and cook on a medium heat for about five minutes, then transfer to a food processor. Process on the pulse button. You may have to add more water or stock to make the mixture whiz. Put back in the saucepan, adding more olive oil (to taste) and adjust the seasoning with lemon juice, salt and pepper. Add the parsley and serve warm, hot or cold.

Roast Loin of Lamb

This marinade can also be used for roast leg of lamb. This cut of meat is very expensive, but definitely worth it for a special occasion. In this recipe, I have used 500g (1lb) to feed 4 people. If the loin has been well trimmed, there will be very little waste. If you are worried about big appetites, serve it with something like the gratin potatoes – which definitely fill you up – although if serving with the lamb, I would leave the cheese topping off. Ideally serve with the potato and rosemary pissaladière (see page 93).

Marinade:
50ml (4 tablespoons) olive oil
50ml (4 tablespoons) Balsamic vinegar
1 teaspoon cumin seed
1 teaspoon fennel seed
1 teaspoon mustard seed
1 tablespoon honey
2 cloves garlic, peeled and crushed
few sprigs thyme
salt and black pepper

500g (1lb) loin of lamb

Preheat oven to 200°C (400°F).

Put all the ingredients for the marinade, except the salt, together in a large bowl or gratin dish and mix well. Add the lamb, cover and marinate overnight if possible.

Before cooking the lamb, bring it to room temperature by taking it out of the fridge and leaving at room temperature for about 15 minutes. Heat a large frying pan, until very hot. Season the lamb generously whilst in the marinade, and carefully place the loin in the pan. Sear on all sides until well browned. Pour in the remaining marinade, transfer to the gratin dish and cook in the oven for a further 12 minutes. Allow to rest – covered – for at least 15 minutes, before slicing and serving.

Chickpea and Aubergine Salad

If you grill the chickpeas for longer, they turn into crunchy and delicious peanut-like snacks – perfect to serve on their own with pre-dinner drinks. You could flavour them up with thyme, garlic or cumin, which you should add at the start of grilling. Alternatively you could just leave them seasoned with salt and pepper.

2 x 400g (14oz) tins cooked
chickpeas, drained
50ml (4 tablespoons) olive oil
salt and black pepper
1 aubergine, diced
1 teaspoon soy sauce
1 teaspoon Hoi-Sin sauce
1 teaspoon sweet chilli sauce
small bunch coriander, finely
chopped
squeeze of lemon juice

Preheat grill to its highest setting.

Place the drained chickpeas on a roasting tray, and pour over half the olive oil. Season with salt and pepper, and grill for about 20 minutes. Cook the chickpeas on a fairly high shelf, but do keep an eye on them. Meanwhile, heat up the remaining olive oil in a large frying pan, and fry the aubergine over a high heat until it starts to brown. The aubergine will absorb the oil very quickly but don't bother adding more as they are like a sponge, and will just end up saturated with oil.

I usually turn down the heat, and add a couple of teaspoons of water. They sizzle, and you can generally give the pan a quick shake, and therefore toss the aubergine around so that it browns more evenly. Add a drop more oil, (but only if you really have to). Turn up the heat again and add the remaining ingredients. Cook for a further five minutes. Check the seasoning and add a squeeze of lemon juice or some more chilli sauce.

Check the chickpeas; when they are slightly crunchy on the outside but still fairly soft in the middle they are ready to be mixed with the aubergine. The chickpeas are quite oily, and that is why you don't want to let the aubergine get too greasy. This is best served warm. Sometimes I like to add baby spinach and a clove of peeled, crushed garlic to the dish while the chickpeas are still warm.

Chicken, Boursin and Parma Ham

This is a dead-easy chicken dish which looks lovely and works very well for a dinner party. It is quite rich, and so should be served with something simple, like a mixed green salad tossed in a good strong vinaigrette. You will need a rolling pin, or some other heavy thick object (no husband or wife gags, please!) to flatten the chicken.

4 chicken breasts, skin removed
2 packs Boursin cheese, sliced
8 thin slices Parma Ham or some
other type of thinly sliced cured
ham such as Serrano
handful basil leaves
salt and pepper
olive oil
100g (4oz) butter

Be very careful about handling other utensils, food or other objects after handling the raw chicken.

WASH YOUR HANDS!

Preheat oven to 200°C (400°F).

First you are going to beat up the chicken breasts. You need to slice them horizontally, but not quite in half. Lay the two attached halves out flat on a large piece of cling film. Fold the cling film over the top of the chicken so it is sandwiched between the cling film. On a chopping board, firmly pound the chicken breasts with the rolling pin so that they spread out and become very thin and flat. Peel the cling film from the top of the chicken and put a quarter of the boursin onto each chicken breast. Place a few basil leaves on top, season lightly and wrap up inside a piece of Parma Ham. Wrap in the cling film and chill until ready to cook. You can leave them overnight, wrapped in the fridge.

Heat up a tablespoon of olive oil in a large frying pan. Have a gratin dish ready. Gently sear the chicken breasts, two at a time, on both sides. Add the butter and baste. Season with plenty of black pepper and transfer to the gratin dish. Providing you have a good golden colour on the chicken and bacon, cover loosely with tin foil, and cook in the oven for about 12 minutes.

If they are looking a bit pale and anaemic, don't bother covering with the foil. Allow to rest for at least three minutes before either slicing, or serving whole. If you are a bit panicky as to whether or not the chicken is cooked, cut one of the breasts in half. If you see pink, put it back in for a few more minutes.

Braised Endive with Blue Cheese

Chicory, witlof, Belgian endive... the list of different names for this edible plant goes on and on. The most common name for it in supermarkets seems to be Belgian endive, as the most common variety available to us hails from this country. It can be eaten raw, either sliced in salads or as a crudite, to be served with dips. The main problem with endive is that it has a tendency towards bitterness. However, this makes it ideal for braising with some sugar or honey before serving with roast meat or game. If you want to elevate this dish, add thin slices of pear which have been dusted with a little sugar, placed on baking paper and carefully grilled. Or you could do the same with walnuts. Serve with some baby spinach leaves and slices of Parma Ham.

1 tablespoon olive oil
4 Belgian endive, sliced in half
salt and pepper
75g (3oz) butter
1 tablespoon sugar
200ml (⅓ pint) stock
200g (7oz) blue cheese, such as Cashel Blue or Roquefort

Preheat oven to 180°C (350°F).

Heat the olive oil in a large frying pan, and sauté the endive (flat side down) for a few minutes over medium-low heat. Season and turn up the heat. Chuck in the butter and sprinkle the sugar on top. Turn the endive over so that they can brown evenly. Allow them to caramelise, then add about a quarter of the stock. Allow most of it to bubble off before transferring the endive and juices to a large gratin dish or roasting tin. Pour in the rest of the stock and cook in the oven, uncovered, for another 15 minutes. If however, the endive are already very brown, then it is best to cover them with tin foil.

Serve the endive on a platter with the blue cheese crumbled on top and some of the cooking juices spooned over.

Sticky Toffee Pudding

I love this recipe – mainly because I am so bad at baking cakes. This pudding is pretty foolproof, improves after a day or two and will win you loads of praise and approval. What more could you ask for? A food processor and a 24cm (10 inch) non-stick cake tin with spring-back sides.

Pudding

375ml (13 fl oz) water

250g (9oz) stoned dates

3 pears, finely diced

150g (5oz) butter

375g (13oz) soft brown sugar

3 eggs, beaten

450g (1lb) plain flour

1 teaspoon baking powder

Toffee and Crème Fraiche Sauce

500ml (18 fl oz) cream

200g (7oz) caster sugar

100g (4oz) soft brown sugar

150g (5oz) butter

400ml (14 fl oz) crème fraiche

Tip: This cake really does improve after a day or two – keep covered in the refrigerator, and simply heat up for 15 minutes (uncovered) at 150°C (300°F) before serving.

Heat the water, dates and pears in a medium-sized saucepan. Bring to the boil then reduce the heat and simmer, until almost all the water has evaporated and the mixture is all soft. This takes about 25 minutes after which it should resemble a purée. Set aside until the pudding bit is made. Preheat oven to 180°C (350°F).

In a food processor, cream the butter and sugar together until light and fluffy. Reduce the speed and add the eggs. Sometimes the mixture separates and starts to look like sour milk. If this happens, add a spoonful of flour and give it a whiz. Pour the mixture into a bowl, and fold in the flour and baking powder. Add the date and pear purée, mix well and pour into the greased 24cm (10 inch) non-stick cake tin with spring back sides. Bake for 45-50 minutes. The sponge should be fairly firm in the centre and a knife should come out clean when inserted in the centre. If not, cover with foil and cook for another 10 minutes. Set aside to cool while you make the toffee sauce.

Heat everything, except for the crème fraiche, in a medium sized saucepan. Bring to the boil, then reduce the heat and simmer for 10 minutes. Remove from the heat, transfer to a bowl and allow to cool for about half an hour. Whisk in the crème fraiche.

Unclip the side of the cake tin and, using a large knife, carefully slice the cake horizontally into two. Put the top half of the pudding on a plate, clip back the cake tin and pour half the toffee sauce onto the bottom half of the pudding. Put the top half back on – pour over any remaining sauce and cover with cling film until ready to serve.

Sautéed Asparagus

Asparagus can take up to five years to cultivate – hence the expensive price, but exquisite taste. I remember once in Holland, an asparagus festival specialising in the delicate, but definitely more anaemic, white variety. For three days we ate nothing but white asparagus with butter, Hollandaise, hard-boiled egg, asparagus soup, gratin... you name it, we ate it. As a result of the overdose, I lean towards the green variety, which definitely has a better and more distinctive flavour.

Two bunches of asparagus will easily feed four people as a starter or side dish.

2 bunches asparagus
generous knob butter
salt and pepper

Trim the stalks of the asparagus and peel any of the tough skin away. There is absolutely no point in telling you how long to cook these for. It will depend on their size, variety and the time of year – but here are the key things to remember. The tips cook much faster, which is why some asparagus fanatics invest in an asparagus steamer. Restaurants tie them in bundles and blanch the bases a little bit longer than the tips.

Either way, I recommend blanching them, (cooking them in boiling water) for about 2-3 minutes. Have a colander ready in the sink. Drain the asparagus in the colander and pour cold running water on to them. Cool completely and eat one. Tender, yet with a little bite is the ideal state. If they are positively crunchy then the next stage will take a bit longer. Alternatively, if they are very soft, the next stage should be brief or left out altogether.

Heat the butter in a large frying pan, add the asparagus and sauté for a minute or two. Season and serve with your favourite dip and olive oil. If you are serving it with the Balsamic and Soy Sauce Dip (on page 64), then go easy on the salt as that dip is very strong

Balsamic and Soy Sauce Dip

I adore this, but have burnt it into oblivion so many times I now force myself to stay in the kitchen (as opposed to wandering off, chatting to friends, them sniffing the air and muttering, "what's that smell?"). Balsamic vinegar is expensive, so it is just an absolute waste of money not to pay attention here – and it only takes a few minutes. This is delicious on just about anything and everything but it gets a bit whiffy when the vinegar heats up – so open a window.

150ml (¼ pint) Balsamic vinegar
50ml (4 tablespoons) soy sauce
1 tablespoon sugar
30g (1oz) butter
black pepper

Put the vinegar and soy sauce in a small saucepan, and bring to the boil. Reduce the heat and gently simmer for about five minutes. Add the sugar and butter. Gently simmer until you have reduced the quantity of liquid by a third. You should end up with 100ml (4 fl oz) of liquid at the end. Season with a little black pepper, and allow to cool before tasting, adjusting the seasoning if necessary. If you want to alter the flavour (if you were serving it with some sort of Asian dish), you could substitute a tablespoon of sesame oil for the butter, and perhaps up the quantity of soy sauce.

Healthy Suppers

Poached Chicken Salad

There is a strong consensus that healthy, low-fat food is dead boring. This kind of dish proves it wrong.

When stir-frying vegetables, I usually use very little oil, and if things sound, smell or look like they're going to burn, just lash in a few tablespoons of water and put a lid on the frying pan. This slows down the cooking and stops things from burning and allows you to cook them a little longer. It's the same idea here, as the chicken is first fried in a fraction of oil until nice and golden. Water or stock is lashed in on top, and a lid goes on. You have the benefit of extra flavouring because of the initial browning stage, yet it remains lovely and moist as the breasts are then poached/steamed.

Drizzle (literally) of olive oil
4 chicken breasts
400ml (¾ pint) water or stock
2cm (1 inch) piece of ginger, peeled and very finely sliced
2 cloves garlic, peeled and crushed
2 tablespoons sweet chilli sauce
1 tablespoon soy sauce
1 tablespoon fish sauce
1 head iceberg lettuce
2 tomatoes, finely diced
small bunch basil and coriander, roughly chopped
wedges of lime to serve

Remember to wash the board, knife and your hands very carefully after you have been prepping raw chicken and before handling any other food or utensils.

Heat the olive oil in a large frying pan. If the chicken breasts have skin, remove this and slice the breast into bite-sized pieces. Fry the chicken, giving the pan a shake if it is sticking. Remember the chicken will stick and then release itself once it has seared sufficiently. Try and get the chicken evenly browned, and then add in about 400ml (¾ pint) water (or stock) along with the ginger, garlic, chilli, fish and soy sauce.

Put the lid on, turn the heat up and bring to the boil, then reduce the heat, remove the lid and cook for a few more minutes. The chicken should be thoroughly cooked by now. Slice the iceberg lettuce and place a few leaves in the centre of each plate. Remove the chicken only, from the pan and divide between the plates.

Put the frying pan back on the heat and boil the sauce over a medium-high heat until it has reduced to a syrupy consistency. Taste for depth of flavour – if the sauce is too strong, you can add a little water. Alternatively if it lacks flavour, reduce it a bit more. Add the tomatoes, basil and coriander. Pour some sauce on to the chicken and serve with extra lemon wedges.

Spiced Beetroot Lentils

Another quick and healthy supper, especially when served with a big bowl of sautéed spinach or goat's cheese grills (see below). I love beetroot salad and roasted beetroot, but find it a pain to cook. The vacuum-packed, ready cooked ones are very handy, and don't taste as briney as the jars of cooked beetroot. Of all the lentil varieties, Puy lentils are a firm favourite of mine. The tinned ones are acceptable, but cooking your own really is delicious. Anyway, for the sake of speed and convenience, I use tinned ones in this recipe. If you want to cook the dried variety, here's what to do:

Allow 400g (14oz) dried Puy lentils for this recipe. Place the lentils in a sieve, and rinse under cold running water. Place in a saucepan and cover with cold water and a spoonful of bicarbonate of soda. Bring the water to the boil, and then drain and rinse. Put them back in the saucepan (no lid on) along with plenty of cold water – the lentils should be generously covered in liquid. Bring to the boil and cook over a low heat for about an hour, or until tender. Drain and rinse. Set aside until ready to use, or cool and refrigerate overnight.

1 teaspoon olive oil

1 onion, peeled and finely diced

salt and freshly ground black pepper

2 x 400g (2 x 14oz) tins chopped peeled tomatoes

2 x 400g (2 x 14oz) tins cooked Puy lentils or above recipe

2 cloves garlic, peeled and finely diced

4 cooked beetroot, finely diced

1 bunch spring onions, finely chopped

pinch cumin

1 tablespoon ketchup

1 tablespoon soy sauce

1 teaspoon sugar

bunch flatleaf parsley, finely chopped

Heat the olive oil in a medium-sized saucepan, and cook the onion for about five minutes over a medium heat until soft. Season lightly. Add all the remaining ingredients (except the parsley which can be added at the last minute), and heat thoroughly for 5-10 minutes. Adjust seasoning and serve in bowls with goat's cheese grills.

Goat's cheese grills: Preheat grill to a high setting, and using some good quality rustic-style bread (raisin and walnut is good) top with 0.5cm (¼ inch) thick slices of goat's cheese, place on a flat baking tray and grill for approximately 5 minutes on second from-the-top shelf until golden brown and bubbling.

Tomato and Wild Rice Goulash

This is one of those dishes that men absolutely hate, unless accompanied by lots of fried meat. OK, OK, not all men – but this is a dreadfully female "I'm going to be wonderfully healthy this week", kind of dish. I like to do double quantities, and keep it for a few days – great for when you don't even have time to chop an onion. My daughter doesn't mind it either which is another advantage, (although I usually have to offer up a little extra ketchup). You can cut out the Worcestershire and soy sauce to really be good, and add lots of chopped fresh tomatoes and extra herbs. I have to confess that I am dreadful at cooking rice. My method may be a technical and purists' nightmare - but it works for me.

Serves 4 as a side dish or 2-3 as a main.

1 teaspoon olive oil
2 onions, peeled and diced
pinch salt
2 x 400g (2 x 14oz) tin chopped, peeled tomatoes
2 teaspoons sugar
50g (2oz) wild rice
200g (7oz) brown rice
500ml (18 fl oz) water
4 cloves garlic, peeled and crushed
1 tablespoon ketchup
1 tablespoon Worcestershire sauce
1 tablespoon soy sauce, optional
large bunch parsley or basil, finely chopped
4 tomatoes, finely diced

Heat the olive oil in a medium sized heavy based saucepan. Add the onions and fry over a medium heat for a good five minutes, until just starting to brown. Don't let them burn – but do let them start to caramelise. Add the salt, tomatoes and sugar. Cook for another 5 minutes. Meanwhile, put both types of rice into a sieve and rinse well under the cold tap. Allow excess water to drain off, and add to the tomatoes. Add the water, garlic, ketchup, Worcestershire and soy sauce.

Bring the rice to the boil, then reduce the heat so that the rice is somewhere between simmering and boiling (an active simmer!). Leave the lid off, but do give the occasional stir to make sure the pan isn't burning. Cook for at least 25 minutes – then put the lid on and turn the heat off. I leave it like this for about 30 minutes. By that stage it will have cooled down sufficiently, so this is a good time to taste and adjust the seasoning. Add the herbs and finely diced tomatoes. Either serve, or allow to cool fully before covering and storing in the fridge up to two days. To reheat, either cover with clingfilm and heat in the microwave, or in a saucepan with a little water.

Low Fat Thai Chicken Soup

The rich taste of a really good Thai chicken soup is sheer indulgence – but can often leave you feeling a little overdosed in the dairy department. Here's a tasty version of that Thai classic which will be very much appreciated by female guests. Take note, boys.

2 chicken stock cubes
2 litres (3½ pints) water
200ml (⅓ pint) reduced fat coconut milk
1cm (½ inch) ginger, peeled and very finely sliced
4-5 lime leaves
4 chicken breasts, sliced into bite size pieces
75g (3oz) water chestnuts
150g (5oz) baby sweetcorn, cut in half
150g (5oz) mangetout, cut in half
200g (7oz) beansprouts
2 red chilli pepper, deseeded and finely chopped
1 tablespoon fish sauce
1 tablespoon soy sauce
1 tablespoon sweet chilli sauce
juice of 1 lime
1 bunch coriander, finely chopped
1 bunch basil, finely chopped

Dissolve the stock cubes in 250ml (½ pint) of boiling water. Then pour into a large saucepan with the remaining 1.75 litres (3 pints) of cold water, along with the coconut milk, ginger and lime leaves. Slowly bring to the boil, and then reduce the heat and add the chicken. Gently simmer for about five minutes and then add the remaining ingredients, except for the herbs. Stir well and cook for another three minutes. Adjust the seasoning if necessary, and throw in the herbs just before serving.

Roast Vegetable Stir Fry

How often have you bought far too many vegetables with great intentions, only to find them rotting in the bottom of the fridge a week later? Once upon a time you might have chucked them out – but not anymore. Pull them all out! Clear the decks! Any combination of these vegetables would do, but obviously try and balance them up. The veg in the first section, require the most cooking – so they would go in first, and the ones in the second section go in second. If you were to use the exact quantities below, you would have loads of veg for 4-6 people as a main course.

Section 1

1 squash or pumpkin
1 courgette, diced
1 aubergine, diced
2 onions, peeled and diced
2 cloves garlic, peeled and crushed
1 sweet potato, diced
2 carrots, peeled and diced
1 tablespoon olive oil
salt and pepper

Section 2

small head of broccoli
1 red pepper deseeded and diced
a handful of green beans, trimmed
a handful mushrooms, peeled and sliced
bunch of asparagus, trimmed
bunch of spring onions, finely chopped
2 tablespoons balsamic vinegar
juice of 1 lemon
2 tablespoons soy sauce
1 tablespoon honey

Preheat oven to 200°C (400°F).

Use as many vegetables as you want from the first section, and place in a large roasting tin. Skin the pumpkin, remove the seeds and roughly chop. Prepare the other vegetables. Pour over the olive oil and mix with you hands, trying to get all the vegetables coated in olive oil. Season generously and roast in the oven for about 15 minutes, uncovered. Take out of the oven, and turn the vegetables over so that they can brown on the other side. Cook for another 10 minutes.

Break the broccoli into small florets, deseed and dice the red pepper and add any other vegetables you want to use from section two, along with the balsamic vinegar, lemon juice, soy sauce and honey. Mix well and roast for another 20 minutes. Take out of the oven and allow to cool slightly before mixing again, checking the seasoning and serving.

This tastes even better a couple of hours after making it, served at room temperature.

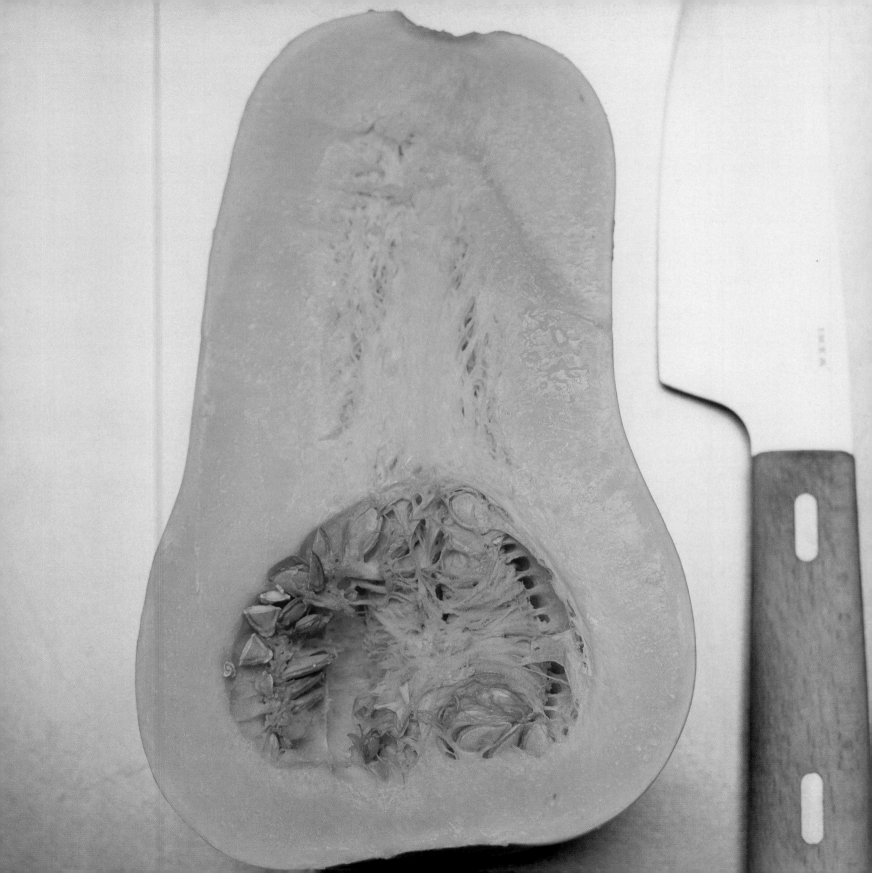

Convenience and Comfort

Convenience and Comfort

Spaghetti with Peas and Smoked Salmon

This is such a safe mid-week supper dish that you can mix and match as much as you like. Vegetarian? No problem – leave out the salmon and substitute some cheese. Hate fish? Grill up some bacon until really crispy and sprinkle on top. There are usually always frozen peas in my freezer – one of the few frozen vegetables that are really decent. Spaghetti, butter and cream are easily bought in local shops. If you are lucky, there may be slices of smoked salmon or bacon. Easy to whip up, and satisfying as hell.

*200g (7oz) spaghetti or
other type of pasta
2 tablespoons olive oil
1 onion, peeled and very finely diced
salt and pepper
1 x 450g (1lb) pack frozen peas
200ml (⅓ pint) cream
1 tablespoon tarragon, finely chopped
200g (7oz) smoked salmon, diced*

Bring a large saucepan of water to boil, and cook the spaghetti for about 9 minutes.

Meanwhile, heat one tablespoon of the olive oil in a medium sized saucepan and fry the onion for a couple of minutes. Season the onion, and then add the cream. Turn up the heat and reduce by boiling gently. Put the peas in another saucepan with about 200ml (⅓ pint) of water. Bring to the boil, simmer for a minute and then drain. Add the tarragon and drained peas to the cream. Turn off the heat and check the seasoning.

Drain the spaghetti, rinse well (with some boiling water – see pasta pointers on page vi) and pour on the other tablespoon of olive oil. Toss the spaghetti and season whilst still in the colander. Put the spaghetti back into the large saucepan and pour on the cream mixture. Add the smoked salmon, mix well and check the seasoning. Serve at once.

Peachie's Puttanesca Sauce

This sauce originated in Italy, where it basically translates as "lady of the night" sauce. These particular working girls used to have a good feed of pasta with puttanesca sauce before a hard night's work. I reckon they used less garlic than we have here so as not to put the punters off...

2 onions, peeled and finely diced
50ml (2oz) olive oil
1 tablespoon sugar
salt and pepper
1 x 400g (14oz) tin peeled, chopped tomatoes
700ml (1 ¼ pints) passata/crushed tomato sauce (or else another 2 x 400g (14oz) tins chopped, peeled tomatoes)
4-6 cloves garlic
1 tablespoon capers
1 tablespoon sweet chilli sauce
1 tablespoon Worcestershire sauce
500g (1lb) buffalo mozzarella, roughly chopped
handful of roughly chopped basil

Sweat the onions in the olive oil over a medium heat. Once they are soft, add the sugar and season with salt and pepper. Add the chopped tomatoes and the passata. Turn the heat down and gently simmer for 10 minutes until the tomatoes have reduced. Add the garlic, capers, chilli and Worcestershire sauce. Stir and cook for a few more minutes. Taste and adjust the seasoning. The sauce will be quite pungent but remember that it has to be strong to flavour the pasta, which is basically tasteless. You can set the sauce aside at this stage.

When you are ready to eat, heat up the sauce and throw in the buffalo mozzarella and basil. Cook for five more minutes over a low heat, until the mozzarella starts to melt. Serve with the cooked pasta of your choice.

Tabouleh

My good friend, Aisling, has long been a maker of this fine salad – which is utterly tasty and in no way resembles the dry, stodgy flavourless muck that is served in many creepy vegetarian cafés. This recipe is wetter than you might expect, but I like it better – there is a real freshness to the flavours. If you aren't watching your weight add a tablespoon of best ever vinaigrette (see page 84) or a splash of fruity extra virgin olive oil. A lot of people would skin and deseed the cucumber for digestive purposes – personally I don't bother. The tabouleh is also gorgeous with coriander and a dash of sweet chilli sauce.

300g (11oz) bulghar wheat
1 teaspoon Marigold stock
or 1 vegetable stock cube and
approximately 450ml water (¾ pint)
4 tomatoes, finely chopped
1 bunch spring onions, finely chopped
1 small cucumber, finely diced
bunch mint, finely chopped
bunch parsley, finely chopped
juice of 1 lemon
2 tablespoons orange juice
(fresh if possible)
black pepper
3 tablespoons Best Ever Vinaigrette
(optional – see page 84)

Boil your kettle. Rinse the bulghar wheat in a sieve under cold running water. Let the excess water drain off then place in a heatproof bowl along with the dry Marigold stock, and enough boiling water to generously cover the bulghar wheat. Cover with cling film and leave to soak for about 30 minutes.

Drain the wheat, and allow all the excess water to drain off. Give the bowl a quick rinse, put the bulghar wheat back in, and add the remaining ingredients. Mix well, check seasoning and serve.

Best Ever Vinaigrette

My sister Peaches has been making this salad dressing for as long as I can remember. She is a great cook, and certainly to blame for my career in food! Many years ago, we started a hamper business selling homemade goods, condiments and dressings. This vinaigrette gained cult status among many lucky recipients. I have tried to bully her into confessing the exact measurements – but as she is such a natural in the kitchen – she just chucks in all the ingredients paying no attention to measurements and quantities. We think this recipe is as close as it gets to her original, turning a big salad into one of my favourite dinners. We love using baby spinach, and making a salad with lots of sliced mushrooms, soft boiled eggs, tomatoes and bacon, or else asparagus, green beans, watercress, mixed lettuce and goat's cheese. Pre-washed lettuce is becoming widely available as retailers recognise consumers need for the super-quick. Still, store dressings always fail to impress me. That's why we make this in one big batch, storing it in an empty olive oil bottle, using it at our leisure. We normally keep this at room temperature, but if you are slow about using it up, keep it in the fridge. More than likely, it'll solidify. Take it out of the fridge an hour before you need it, or else dunk the bottle into a bowl of hot water for a minute or two. It'll soon become liquid enough to shake and use.

500ml (19 fl oz) olive oil
100ml (4 fl oz) Balsamic vinegar
120ml (5 fl oz) white wine vinegar
4 cloves garlic, peeled and crushed
2 tablespoons English mustard
2 tablespoons ketchup
2 tablespoons soy sauce
3 tablespoons honey
2 tablespoons Worcestershire sauce
salt and black pepper

Whiz all the ingredients together in a blender. Season very well.
Store in the fridge for three to four weeks.

Canapés
Starters
Party Food

Canapés
Starters
Party Food

Artichoke Dip

This recipe was given to my sister by a childhood friend. I have always been eternally grateful for this crowd-pleaser. People love this kind of party food – especially the golden brown melted cheese on top. If you were having a dinner party, you could always do this in individual ramekins for a très posh effect. Although it is basically vegetarian, don't forget that Worcestershire sauce contains anchovies. Staunch herbivores should be warned.

Easily feed 10 for canapés, or 4-6 as individual starters.

*3 x 400g (14oz) tins whole
artichoke hearts, drained
1 onion, finely diced
200g (7oz) mayonnaise
200g (7oz) grated cheese – Gruyere
and mozzarella are good
1 tablespoon Worcestershire sauce
1 tablespoon wholegrain mustard
salt and freshly ground black pepper*

Preheat the oven to 180°C (350°F).

Drain the artichokes well, or the dip will be very soggy.

Chop the artichokes very finely and mix in a large ovenproof bowl, or gratin dish, with the onion, mayonnaise, half of the grated cheese and remaining ingredients. Taste and adjust seasoning if necessary; you may want to add more mayonnaise. Smooth the top of the dip and top with the remaining grated cheese.

Cook for about 30 minutes, until the topping is golden brown, and the dip is piping hot. Serve with your favourite crackers.

Rare Beef Skewers

These are always wolfed down at parties – they are very 'moreish' and although expensive, there is absolutely no waste. Perfect for small, special gatherings, but definitely not to be served to dreadful in-laws. Makes enough skewers for about 10 people. They don't really need any dipping sauce – but you can always serve with some aioli, (see page 101) sweet chilli sauce, or the reduced Balsamic and Soy Sauce Dip (see page 64).

The beef can be cooked ahead of time and then reheated in a moderate oven and skewered. These are particularly nice if marinated overnight. But if you can't, don't worry – they will still taste great. If you want to cook them on the barbecue, soak the wooden skewers overnight in water, drain and skewer the raw beef, then cook on a hot barbecue for about five minutes. Allow to rest for a few minutes and then serve.

500g (1 lb) fillet of beef
1 tablespoon soy sauce
1 tablespoon Worcestershire sauce
1 tablespoon tomato ketchup
1 tablespoon sugar
salt and freshly ground black pepper
1 tablespoon olive oil

Make sure the fillet is completely trimmed and free of any white sinew. Cut into 2cm (1 inch) chunks. Mix together the soy, Worcestershire sauce, tomato ketchup and sugar. Marinate the beef in this for up to 24 hours.

When you are ready to cook the meat, heat the olive oil in a medium sized saucepan until it is very hot and smoking. Season the beef generously, then fry it over a very high heat for about two minutes in total. Initially it will stick to the pan, but it will gradually release itself. Once it has stopped sticking, toss around the pan so that the beef is well coated in the marinade, and then transfer to a plate. It will cook very fast, especially if served rare.

When the beef is just cool enough to handle, thread a couple of pieces onto wooden or metal skewers and serve.

Rosemary and Potato Pissaladière

Although puff pastry is a bore-chore to make, it is to die for if you have time. But the commercial stuff isn't too bad. Ready-made puff pastry sheets are readily available in the freezer section of most supermarkets. Just take out a sheet a few hours or the night before you want to use it, so the pastry has time to thaw out. Then you will only have to roll it out with a little flour. This pissaladière goes so well with the roast lamb on page 53. It makes a welcome change from serving spuds and looks like you've gone to huge effort and trouble. It is also great as a supper or lunchtime dish, especially if served with some good cheese and a salad. Any large type of spud will do, although Roosters, with their gorgeous purple skin, are especially nice to use. It is best to make this in a large baking tray.

*1 sheet ready made puff pastry,
fully thawed out
2 potatoes, very finely sliced
4 sprigs rosemary or thyme
2 tablespoons olive oil
salt and black pepper
a few Parmesan shavings, optional*

Preheat oven to 180°C (350°F).

Roll out the puff pastry so that it is a good 2cm (1 inch) wider and longer than the baking tray. Place the sheet of pastry on to the baking tray. Lightly press into the corners and trim away the excess pastry that is hanging over the edges.

Layer the potatoes in neat rows on top of the pastry, overlapping only slightly. If there are too many potatoes, the pastry won't cook thoroughly. Top with sprigs of rosemary and evenly pour over the olive oil. Season well and bake for about 25-30 minutes until the potatoes are golden brown. If they look like they are starting to burn, cover them in tin foil. Top with Parmesan shavings. Slice and serve.

Grilled Mushrooms with Manchego

A hint of Barcelona – courtesy of the Manchego cheese – but most hard types of cheese such as Parmesan or Asciago would do. The breadcrumbs stop this dish from turning into a riverlet of olive oil. A good starter.

4 large field mushrooms
4 generous tablespoons pesto
2 tablespoons white bread crumbs
150g (5oz) Manchego cheese,
thinly sliced

Preheat the grill to its highest setting.

Don't wash the mushrooms. Peel off the outer skin in strips – start by pulling the outer layer from under the mushroom and gently pull the strip towards the top. Carefully snap off the stem, and put the mushrooms on a baking or roasting tray.

Mix the pesto with the breadcrumbs, and divide the mixture between the mushrooms. Top with the Manchego and grill for about 5-7 minutes until the cheese is starting to bubble and the mushrooms are heated through. Serve on its own or with some of the balsamic and soy sauce dip (see page 64) drizzled over the plate with some lettuce and crusty bread.

Pesto

You can use any type of nut you like for making pesto. I like using a combination of pine and pistachio nuts, but walnuts are also good especially if you are serving it with chicken. Swap around herbs as well – sometimes people use rocket or coriander, but I find so much of the rocket now available in supermarkets is bitter and overpriced.

100g (4oz) pack basil
6 cloves garlic, peeled
100g (4oz) pistachio nuts, shelled
50g (2oz) pine nuts
1 teaspoon caster sugar
salt and freshly ground black pepper
50g (2oz) grated Parmesan cheese
300ml (½ pint) olive oil

Put all the ingredients except the olive oil, into a food processor and process until the mixture is as smooth as you want it. I prefer to leave it on the chunky side, so tend to process the pesto using the pulse button on my machine. Add as much olive oil as you like, depending on what you are using it for. If the pesto is for a pasta sauce, then you may want to use all the oil – but if you are using it for the stuffed mushrooms, leave it a little thicker.

Meatballs with Tomato and Chorizo Sauce

A really tasty and piquant treat – best served as a starter as it can be a bit overpowering when served as a main course. You will need some good crusty bread to mop up all the juices. If you can't get chorizo, you can substitute another cured type of sausage or leave it out entirely. The chorizo adds body and depth to the sauce, but is not absolutely vital.

First you have to make the tomato sauce and allow it to reduce and develop in flavour. Then the meatballs are fried separately in a little olive oil. This browning of the meat is important for two reasons; first, it helps cement their shape – if you tried to cook meatballs in a liquid tomato sauce, they would disintegrate and it would just become a sort of bolognaise mess; second, browning, searing and sealing gives flavour to meat. And we love to give flavour...

2 tablespoons olive oil
1 onion, peeled and finely diced
2 x 400g (14oz) tins peeled,
chopped tomatoes
2-3 cloves garlic, peeled and crushed
1 tablespoon ketchup
1 tablespoon Worcestershire sauce
little splash, Tabasco sauce
2 chorizo sausages, sliced into 1cm
(½ inch) rounds.
500g minced beef
salt and pepper
few basil leaves, to garnish

Heat a tablespoon of olive oil in a medium sized saucepan and when soft, add the tomatoes. Turn the heat up and reduce the liquid. After five minutes, add the garlic, ketchup, Worcestershire sauce and Tabasco. Taste and adjust the seasoning if necessary. The sauce can be allowed to cool fully then chilled overnight, until you are ready to cook the meatballs and serve.

Gently simmer the tomato sauce. Season the mince with salt and pepper, then take tablespoons of mince and roll them into small balls. Set aside on a plate and heat the second tablespoon of olive oil in a large frying pan. Fry about 4–5 meatballs at a time. Gently place them in the pan and don't move them for about a minute. The meat will stick to the pan and then eventually release itself when ready. Try to brown them evenly on all sides – but be gentle or they will fall apart. When they are evenly browned, transfer to the simmering tomato sauce. Cook for a further 10 minutes over a low heat, until the mince is fully cooked, and all the flavours have developed. Serve in small bowls with warm crusty bread to accompany and a few basil leaves on top.

Potato Croquettes with Aioli

Another reminder of dear old Barcelona and the restaurants that line the harbour with their canvas canopies and waiters in stiff white shirts fussing over tanned, glamorous customers. During the course of one particularly lazy afternoon lunch, we steadily ordered a bunch of starters that were more substantial than tapas, though not quite starters. A constant stream of food arrived, including sautéed razor clams, meatballs, chorizo and the most delicious potato croquettes, so good that we ordered extra portions.

After some experimenting, I realised that the "cheesy" texture was coming from the aioli/mayonnaise mixed in with the potatoes before they were deep-fried. The added protein enriches them, but also gives them a lightness you just wouldn't get with cheese. The croquettes are easily shallow fried – just watch that the oil doesn't get too grubby with burnt breadcrumbs. Err on the side of lightly frying them. Keep the cooked croquettes warm in a gratin dish in the oven while you finish the whole batch.

4 large potatoes, peeled and cut into 2cm (1 inch) cubes
5 tablespoons aioli
2 tablespoons mayonnaise
3 slices Parma ham, finely sliced (optional)
3 eggs, beaten
salt and black pepper
4 slices white bread, made into breadcrumbs
oil, for shallow frying

extra aioli to serve

See page 101 for Aioli recipe. Cook the potatoes in boiling water until tender. Drain and put back in the saucepan over a low heat. Cover with a tea towel, and "steam" for a minute to help the potatoes dry out. Allow to cool slightly and then mash. Let the potatoes cool fully before you mix with the aioli, mayonnaise and Parma ham. Taste and season if necessary. At this stage, you can shape them into small balls or croquette shapes (the balls are easier). They can be left overnight until you are ready to fry them.

To finish, set up a little assembly line. Turn the oven on low (about 130°C (250°F)), heat up about 0.5cm (¼ inch) of oil in a large frying pan. Have the bowl of beaten egg ready, with the bowl of breadcrumbs next in line, followed by a clean empty plate.

Place an ovenproof gratin dish beside the cooker. Have a slotted spoon ready – and away you go.

Put about two or three balls at a time into the egg. Using your hands, gently lift them out of the egg bath and into the breadcrumb bowl. Lightly coat and transfer to the clean plate. Repeat until all the balls have been crumbed. It gets a bit tricky at the end, simply because globs of egg have ended up in the breadcrumb bowl, so your final few always look a bit the worse for wear. At this stage, clean up your hands, and get rid of the assembly line clutter. Check the oil is hot, but certainly not smoking. Drop a few breadcrumbs into the oil – it should take about 10-15 seconds for them to brown.

Carefully fry the croquettes until they are golden brown. You will have to turn them over so that they are browned on all sides. Transfer to the gratin dish and continue until all the croquettes are done. They will be fine left covered in the oven for 15-20 minutes. Any longer and the mayonnaise and aioli will start to leak out of the croquettes. Serve with extra aioli.

Aioli

Totally and utterly addictive! No one will want to kiss you after you've had a few bites of this – so you need to get some into your loved one first. I adore this with anything – seared tuna, asparagus, potatoes, rare beef... – the list is endless. You can just use olive oil if you like, but it can be a little overbearing – similarly, using all vegetable oil can be very bland.

4 egg yolks
1 teaspoon salt
1 teaspoon caster sugar
6 cloves garlic, peeled
juice of 1 lemon
200ml (⅓ pint) olive oil
100ml (4 fl oz) vegetable oil

In a food processor, mix the egg yolks with the salt, sugar, garlic and lemon. When smooth, leave the motor running on a medium speed, and start pouring the olive oil in – slowly. The mixture should start to emulsify; becoming noticeably thicker. If you are not sure what is happening, stop the machine to take a look and give it a stir with a spoon. Turn the motor back on and continue pouring in the remaining olive and vegetable oil. The mixture should be thick (like mayonnaise). Taste and adjust seasoning if necessary. Can be stored in the fridge for a few days – but it usually disappears after a day!

Herb Chicken with Romesco Sauce

This sauce may sound a bit dreary, but after one bite you'll be hooked. It is strong and packed with flavour – perfect with prawns, grilled fish, grilled chicken or roast vegetables. If you have a food processor, it'll only take a few minutes to make. I make it with jars of sweet piquante peppers, available in most supermarkets. If you can't find these, you could always use some roasted red peppers, adding some chilli to give it a lift. The sauce will keep covered in the fridge for a week. You could also add a spoon of sauce to some cooked pasta and toss with lots of chopped fresh tomatoes and plenty of fresh herbs.

1 x 375g (13oz) jar sweet piquante peppers, drained
150g (5oz) pine nuts
8 cloves garlic, peeled
1 teaspoon smoked paprika
salt and pepper
200ml (⅓ pint) olive oil

Process everything except the olive oil in the food processor until it turns into a smooth paste. Leave the motor running, on a low-ish setting and slowly pour in the olive oil. Once all the ingredients are well mixed, check the seasoning. Pour into a bowl and serve with the herb chicken.

4 chicken breasts
50ml (4 tablespoons) olive oil
salt and black pepper
few sprigs rosemary and thyme
50g (2oz) butter

Remove the skin from the chicken breasts and slice into 2cm (1 inch) thick slices. Wash your hands, knife and chopping board very carefully before handling anything else. Heat the olive oil in a large frying pan or chargrill pan. When the pan is very hot, fry the chicken on both sides. Remember not to force the chicken to flip over if stuck to the pan – when it is good and brown it will release itself and that is the time to turn it over. Season generously, add the herbs and add in the butter. Cook over a high heat for another couple of minutes until the chicken is golden brown and cooked through. Either serve straight away with the Romesco sauce, or transfer to a gratin dish and cover with tin foil; it will be okay for about 20-30 minutes in a low oven (130°C (250°F)).

Courgette, Red Pepper and Anchovy Egg Rolls

This reminds me so much of Barcelona and the many delicious tapas bars that inundate that city. Greed is often the greatest incentive to try some of the stranger varieties of tapas – but this one is pretty straightforward. Many anti-anchovy fanatics will actually tolerate them here. Feel free to add some chopped parsley or other herbs. Don't bother trying to make this in anything other than a non-stick pan.

10 eggs, beaten
2 courgettes, grated
2 red pepper, grated
1 small tin anchovies
100g (4oz) butter

You are going to fry the eggs in three batches. Heat a third of the butter, allow it to melt and foam over a medium heat and pour in a third of the beaten eggs. Have a large flat plate ready. Swirl the eggs around the pan so that the egg mixture evenly covers the base. Sprinkle a third of both the grated courgette and grated red pepper evenly over the egg. Add a third of the anchovies and drizzle with a tiny bit of anchovy oil from the tin. Lower the heat and cook for about five minutes until the egg starts to solidify.

If you have lots of liquid bits on top, push some of the egg mixture back from the outside edge of the pan towards the centre with a wooden spoon. Tip the pan so that anything runny can take the place of the egg you have just pushed back. Give the pan a little shake. The egg should move as a solid whole piece, as opposed to ripping and falling to pieces. Once you are confident that the egg is cooked and will slide onto the plate – go ahead and DO IT!

Wipe out the pan, with a little kitchen paper but don't bother washing it out. Melt a little more butter, and repeat the process two more times. At the end (hopefully) you should have three flat "pancakes" stacked on top of each other. Cut them into slices or squares, or else roll them up and slice into 2cm (1 inch) rolls, which can be served as canapés.

Spiced Sausage Cakes

These are so tasty – we served them at a large canapé party and our waiters were literally mobbed. It is important to use decent sausage meat but I did make this once from really cheap sausages (skin and all) and we all survived. Obviously the nicer the sausage meat, the nicer the end result. If you are using a particular brand of sausages that are very salty, leave out the soy sauce. These make about 16 small patties, which would be a generous starter for 4-5 people.

500g (1lb) good quality sausages, or sausage meat
1 tablespoon soy sauce
2 tablespoon sweet chilli sauce
2 cloves garlic, peeled and crushed
Small bunch coriander, roughly chopped
Approx. 50ml (4 tablespoons) vegetable oil, for frying
Flour for dusting

Preheat oven to 180°C (350°F).

Put the sausages, soy and sweet chilli sauces, garlic and coriander into a food processor and process until well mixed. Transfer to a bowl, and taking generous spoonfuls of the sausage mixture, shape into little patty shapes. Dust with flour and transfer to a clean plate. Once you have reached this stage, you can either leave the uncooked sausage cakes refrigerated for a few hours, or cook them straight away.

To cook them, heat up about half the oil in a large frying pan. When the oil is hot (i.e. a good sizzling sound erupts from the pan when you carefully put one of the sausage cakes in), put about half the cakes into the pan with a slotted spoon – don't overcrowd them. You may have to cook them in three batches. Have a roasting tin or gratin dish ready. Fry the cakes for a few minutes on both sides until well browned. Transfer to the gratin dish, fry the remaining cakes and then cook in the oven, covered with tin foil for 15-25 minutes, depending on how thick the cakes are. Serve with extra sweet chilli sauce mixed with some soy sauce, sesame oil and coriander. Garnish with slices of chilli and extra sprigs of coriander.

Kids
Dinners

Kids' Dinners

Yummy Mummy Pasta Sauce

The following quantity makes enough to fill a 500g (1lb) jar, plus a bit extra. The basic principle here is to put it all in, and either use it up within a couple of days, or make a double quantity and freeze some in plastic containers. Even if you end up defrosting the sauce in the microwave, you can at least boil up some penne or spaghetti and hey presto, you have a super healthy dinner that is not even too bad for adults. Go on, eat those greens! Be super good, and use as many organic vegetables as possible.

4 carrots, peeled,
2 courgettes
2 sticks celery
8 tomatoes
2 cloves garlic, peeled and crushed
2 sweet potatoes
2 red onions
1 bunch parsley
2 tablespoons olive oil

Peel, wash and chop up the vegetables as roughly as you like. Heat the olive oil in a large saucepan, and add everything in. Cover with a lid, cook until soft, and then purée in a food processor. Use the sauce straight away or else cool, transfer into plastic containers and freeze. It's fine in the freezer for a month or two. Simply thaw out and heat in a small saucepan with a little water, and check the seasoning. Basically, it is great to do this sauce with no salt – goodness knows we eat far too much.

Fish and Chips

Cooking your own fried fish is so delicious, it is worth every succulent bite. I use a whole combination of fish for this – plaice, cod or sole all work well. Skin the fish, then have a good feel around for any bones that can be pulled out using a tweezers before you cut the fish into strips or chunks. To do chips really well is quite tricky, as so much depends on starch and sugar content, as well as age and variety of the potatoes. This is why for home cooking, I like to do them like this. It is fairly hassle-free, and results are dependable.

4 – 6 Desiree or Maris Piper potatoes
(total weight around 1kg (2lb))
vegetable oil (about 500ml (18 fl oz))
250g (9oz) butter
salt and black pepper
600g (1lb 5oz) fish fillets, skinned and
cut into chunks
2 eggs, beaten
approximately 100-200g (4-8oz) flour
(for dusting)

Preheat oven to 160°C (310°F).

Slice the potatoes into 1cm (½ inch) thick slices or chip shapes. Pat dry with kitchen paper. Heat half the vegetable oil and all of the butter in a large frying pan. Carefully add the potatoes to the hot fat with a slotted spoon or other suitable utensil. Cook over a medium-high heat until the potatoes are starting to turn golden. Remove from the heat and transfer the potatoes to a roasting tin. Carefully pour in the hot fat, and cook in the oven for about 30 minutes, until the potatoes are golden brown and cooked through. Remove from the roasting tin on to kitchen paper. Pat excess oil away and season generously. These will keep warm in the oven for about 20 minutes at 120°C (240°F).

You can prep the fish about 30 minutes in advance. Set up a little assembly line starting with the fish, then the bowl of beaten eggs, followed by a bowl of flour (seasoned with salt and pepper), and ending with a clean plate. Dip the pieces of fish into the beaten egg, then toss lightly with flour and set aside onto the clean plate. Cover with clingfilm and refrigerate for up to 30 minutes until you are ready to start frying.

Get a plate ready with lots of kitchen paper to hand. Heat up the remaining oil in a medium sized saucepan (it should be at a 2-3cm (1-1 ½ inch) level in the saucepan), and add the fish in small batches. Cook for about 3-4 minutes, until the outside is golden brown. If the fish is browning too much, reduce the heat. Only cook a few pieces at a time or the pan will get overcrowded and the fish will not crisp. Drain on kitchen paper, season well and serve with the chips and pea purée (see page 114).

Pea Purée

The words "pea purée" fill me with dread when I see them on restaurant menus. For some reason I imagine a revolting mush of tinned processed peas, tasting vaguely of metal. This, on the other hand, is such a sumptuous sauce, ridiculously easy and truly moreish. Frozen peas are totally acceptable, as far as frozen fruit and veg go. Some chefs would even argue that they like using them a whole lot better than the fresh stuff.

1 x 450g (1lb) bag of frozen peas
50g (2oz) butter
1 onion, peeled and finely diced
100ml (4 fl oz) cream
salt and black pepper
small bunch mint

Heat up the frozen peas with enough water to cover in a medium sized saucepan. Bring the water to the boil and break up the lumps of frozen peas. When they have defrosted and are hot through (this will only take 2-3 minutes), drain and put into a food processor or blender. Meanwhile, sauté the butter and onion together until soft over a low heat. Take your time and don't let the onion brown.

When the onions are ready, add them to the peas along with the remaining ingredients. Process until smooth. Taste and adjust seasoning if necessary. This can be made a day in advance, covered and stored overnight in the fridge. Reheat the purée in a saucepan before serving with a little extra cream or splash of water if it has dried out in the fridge

Fancy Fish Burger

My friend Caroline was "Queen of the Fishburgers" when we were teenagers. These were elaborate affairs: two pieces of toast with red cheddar melted on one side, topped with three perfectly grilled fish fingers, garden lettuce, sliced tomato, onion and beetroot (yes, beetroot). A good dollop of mayonnaise and ketchup completed the dish. Oddly enough, they were quite fabulous. Tastes are a little more refined nowadays. Fresh cod has replaced the fish fingers and the beetroot has taken a hike.

4 x cod fillets each weighing 150g (5oz), skin removed
1-2 tablespoons olive oil
salt and black pepper
50g (2oz) butter
salt and pepper
2 tablespoons chopped flatleaf parsley
4 x baps
2 tomatoes, sliced
handful of mache or other delicate lettuce
4 tablespoons good quality tartare sauce
lemon wedges to serve

Preheat oven to 150°C (300°F).

Heat half the olive oil in a large frying pan, season the cod and cook two fillets at a time so as not to overcrowd the pan. After three minutes on a medium heat, add half the butter and half the parsley. Flip the fillets over, season the other side (if you haven't already done so), and after another two minutes, transfer to a gratin dish or roasting tin. Pour the butter and oil from the pan into the roasting tin, and repeat the frying process with the remaining olive oil, fillets and butter. Cover the fish with tin foil and place in the oven while you assemble the rest, (this takes about 10 minutes). The parsley will go quite crispy in the frying pan. If you are a fan of parsley, you can always fry a little more in some of the oil and butter, as it is delicious on top of the fish.

Toast the baps and butter the bottom half. Place the bottom half in the centre of each plate. Layer the sliced tomatoes and mache lettuce. Remove the cod from the oven and place a fillet on top of each bap. Spread some tartare sauce onto the top half of the baps, and place beside the fish burgers. Leave the burgers open so that guests can squeeze some lemon onto their fish before closing up the burgers with the top half of the bap.

Hamburger Night

Hamburgers are just the business. They are also VERY, VERY easy. Although I love the barbecue, for some reason I can't cook burgers this way. I can barbecue chicken and large tenderloins of beef very well, but fish and burgers are just a disaster for me. I prefer to do them in a pan, where the temperature is easily controlled. I have perfected the art of the indoor home burger – the important thing is to have the grill very hot (for grilling the cheese, at the end), and make sure your pan is smoking. Serve with all your favourites – mine include fried mushrooms, caramelised onions, and crispy bacon with Swiss cheese. I don't bother with buns, but I really do try and encourage people to buy organic mince.

800g (1¾ lb) organic minced beef

2 eggs

2 tablespoons ketchup

1 teaspoon salt

1 tablespoon Dijon mustard

1 tablespoon Worcestershire sauce

few dashes of Tabasco sauce

1 tablespoon chopped parsley

1 medium red onion, peeled and very finely chopped

olive oil

100g (4oz) butter

4 slices of Swiss, cheddar or any other favourite cheese

Throw all the ingredients into a bowl, except for the oil, butter and cheese. Mix well and chill. At this stage, you can shape them into 4 burgers, cover in cling film and leave in the fridge for an hour. If you want to leave them for a few hours longer, then leave out the salt and season them at the last minute.

Preheat the grill to its highest setting. Heat some olive oil in the frying pan until smoking. Gently fry two burgers at a time for about two minutes and then flip over. They should have a good colour. If not, you are wussing out and that pan was not hot enough! After another minute add half the butter and baste. Transfer to a gratin dish. Add a bit more oil to the frying pan and fry the remaining burgers. When you have all four burgers in the gratin dish, top with cheese, and grill for about 4 minutes. They will still be medium rare inside. Cook for another 8 minutes if you want them well done.

Serve with your favourite garnishes – pickles, mustard, ketchup, mayonnaise, raw onion, sliced tomatoes…

Sunday
Lunch

Sunday Lunch

Roast Chicken with Tarragon Gravy

Contrary to kitchen myth, roasting meat does not take ages, is far from complicated and does not leave a trail of dirty pots and pans. A medium roast chicken serves 3-4 people (depending on how savage your guests are) and besides being incredibly satisfying, is also ridiculously easy.

1 medium chicken, approx 1.5kg (3lb)
1 lemon, cut in half
5 cloves garlic, unpeeled
salt and pepper
1 tablespoon honey
1 tablespoon Worcestershire sauce
1 tablespoon Dijon mustard
about 200ml (⅓ pint) of stock or water
or a glass of white wine
small bunch finely chopped tarragon

Preheat oven to 200ºC (400ºF). Rinse the chicken in cold water, and place in a roasting tray – don't worry if it's wet. Stick half the lemon and all of the garlic inside the bird, and squeeze the other lemon half over the chicken. Season generously. Cover in tin foil, and roast for about 45 minutes. Then remove the foil and cook for about another 15 minutes. At this stage, take it out and leave for a few minutes. Give the legs a wiggle – they should move about freely, and then slice between the leg and the breast. Check what colour it is. It shouldn't be too pink, and the juices should be clear. If it looks nearly done, shove it back in the oven, with the tin foil wrapped around it, turn the oven off, have a glass of wine, and when you are done, the chicken will be too.

Boil up your kettle. Remove the bird, and carve it up. I start with the legs, then the wings, then slice up the breast. Lay it all out on a big plate then make your gravy. Pour some of the boiling water from the kettle onto the roasting tray – this will help dissolve all those delicious meat juices, (and help with the washing up), and scrape with a wooden spoon. If you can put the roasting tray on to direct heat, great, if not pour the contents into a saucepan. Add the honey and remaining ingredients. If you have the garlic cloves from the inside the chicken, squeeze them into the mixture. If not, add a clove of fresh, crushed garlic. Heat thoroughly and taste. If it is a bit watery, turn up the heat and reduce by boiling for a minute or two. Alternatively, add some more water or stock if it gets too thick. Pour into a jug and serve with the chicken.

Roast Rib of Beef

There is something ultimately satisfying about a big rib of beef, plainly roasted with lashings of salt, black pepper and thyme. The crispy outside is always the bit that gets hacked off by greedy guests, before carving begins. I love having this dish with Gratin Potatoes (see page 42) or Two Way Warm Potato Salad (see page 126). Or splash out and make the Hollandaise from the Eggs Benedict recipe (see page 2), adding a tablespoon of chopped tarragon to make a Sauce Béarnaise. A rib roast is considered by many to be the most suitable cut of beef for roasting. It is better to roast it on the bone, but carving it can be tricky and an arduous task for the inexperienced. So, here is a recipe for no-bone roasting! Rib of beef is widely available in supermarkets already boned and rolled for your convenience, and the weight is on the package. Allow 250g (8oz) of meat (without the bone), per person.

1kg (2lb) rib of beef, rib
bones removed
1 tablespoon olive oil
salt and black pepper
few sprigs thyme

Preheat oven to 180°C (350°F).

Put the beef in a large roasting tray and rub the surface of the beef with the olive oil, using your hands. Wash your hands!

Season the meat generously with salt, lots of black pepper and thyme. Roast for about 40 minutes uncovered, for rare to medium rare. Remove the beef from the oven and allow the beef to rest somewhere warm, covered in tin foil for about 20 minutes before carving. Carve medium thick slices (about 1.5cm (1 inch) thick) and serve with your favourite vegetables. If you like beef medium or medium well, simply roast for 20 minutes longer.

125

Two Way Warm Potato Salad

Both of these are quick 'n' easy, good for buffets or relaxed dinner parties. The salt may seem excessive, but it's necessary. This is one recipe that needs very good quality olive oil – and be sure to add the olive oil and garlic while the potatoes are still warm. Cooking potatoes and rice are two things I always manage to get wrong. Even if the potatoes are overcooked and end up more like mash – it doesn't matter. It will still taste good.

1.5kg (3 ½ lb) potatoes, peeled and diced into 2cm (1 inch) pieces
2 onions, peeled and finely sliced
50g (2oz) butter
1 teaspoon paprika
1 teaspoon salt
freshly ground black pepper
150ml (¼ pint) olive oil
4 cloves garlic, peeled and crushed
1 bunch flatleaf parsley, finely chopped

Cook the potatoes for about ten minutes in boiling water until tender. Meanwhile, sauté the onions in the butter and add the paprika. Season with half of the salt and lots of black pepper. When the potatoes are ready, drain and separate into two bowls. In one, add the paprika and onion mixture with half of the olive oil. Mix well and adjust seasoning. In the other bowl add the remaining olive oil, the remaining salt, the crushed garlic and the parsley. Check the seasoning and allow both salads to absorb all the flavours for about 30 minutes before serving. If you feel that the potatoes are a bit dry, add more olive oil and a squeeze of lemon juice.

Lasagne

Layer upon layer of tastiness. The key is to have each layer superbly seasoned so that they could almost be served on their own. Too often, people make boring béchamel or a watery meat sauce. They don't bother draining the spinach enough either, and the end product becomes a dripping mass of nastiness. This would happily feed approximately 6-8 grateful guests – grateful for all your efforts to keep the layers high 'n dry and mighty tasty.

To fit a medium sized roasting tin.

450g (1lb) bag of frozen spinach
250g (9oz) tub of mascarpone
50ml (4 tablespoons) olive oil
1kg (2lb) minced meat
salt and pepper
3 onions, finely diced
3 x 400g (14oz) tins of peeled chopped tomatoes
4 cloves garlic, peeled and crushed
2 tablespoons Worcestershire sauce
½ teaspoon smoked paprika
1 tablespoon soy sauce
2 teaspoons sugar
1 bunch flat parsley, finely chopped

Defrost the spinach in the microwave or in a saucepan over a gentle heat as per cooking instructions on the packet. Drain, using a sieve, and don't be afraid to squeeze out any excess liquid. Mix with the mascarpone, season and set aside.

Heat half the olive oil in a large frying pan until good and hot. Cook the mince over a high heat until well browned and season well. This should take about 12-15 minutes. Have a colander ready, pour the mince into it and drain. Set aside and start making the tomato sauce.

Heat the remaining olive oil in a large saucepan and sweat the onions until soft. Season, and add the tomatoes. Cook over a high heat to reduce the mixture. After about five minutes add the remaining ingredients and the drained meat. Reduce the heat and cook for 20 minutes until the mince is fully cooked. Check the seasoning and adjust if necessary. Set aside and make the béchamel.

Béchamel

100g (4oz) butter
100g (4oz) flour
600ml (1 pint) milk
salt and pepper

250g (9oz) grated cheese (such as
mozzarella, cheddar)

Melt the butter in a medium sized saucepan, add the flour and stir vigorously. It will go all lumpy and start to resemble polenta (this is called a roux). Cook over a gentle heat for two minutes – try not to let the saucepan burn. If the roux is starting to brown, remove from the heat and keep stirring. It is really important to cook the roux for this period of time, otherwise the béchamel will taste of uncooked flour. Add a good splash of milk, and mix vigorously with a whisk. It will go all lumpy, but just keep whisking. Add more milk after each bit becomes incorporated and keep heating gently. When all the milk is added, cook for a further 5 minutes, stirring gently, ensuring the bottom of the pan is not burning. Add the grated cheese (thus the béchamel now becomes a cheese sauce), stir and set aside. You are now ready to assemble the lasagne.

Put a layer of mince at the bottom of the roasting tin, or large casserole dish. Top with one layer of lasagne sheets, then the spinach layer. Pour the cheese sauce directly onto the spinach. Either allow to cool fully and refrigerate for up to 24 hours, or else cook for 45-60 minutes at 180°C (350°F). Remove from the oven and allow to rest for 10 minutes before slicing and serving.

Chicken, Leek and Blue Cheese Pie

This is perfect for supper on a cold and wintery night or late Sunday lunch. Ready-made puff pastry is grand to use especially for things like savoury pies. Roll out the pastry until it is a third bigger than its original size, using a rolling pin, a good sprinkling of flour and a clean flat surface.

Béchamel

100g (4oz) butter
100g (4oz) flour
600ml (1 pint) milk
salt and pepper

Filling

2 tablespoons olive oil
3 chicken breasts, cut into bite sized pieces
100g (4oz) butter
3-4 leeks, washed and sliced
3 large field mushrooms, peeled and chopped
150g (5oz) blue cheese
1 sheet ready-made puff pastry

To make the béchamel, see page 128. Season and set aside. You can do this at least 24 hours in advance.

Heat up one tablespoon of olive oil in a saucepan and cook the chicken pieces over a high heat until they start to colour. Season, and add half the butter. Cook for a further 5 minutes over a medium heat. When fully cooked, transfer to the casserole dish, spreading the chicken pieces out evenly on the base. Put the saucepan back on the heat and add the remaining tablespoon olive oil. Fry the leek and mushrooms. Season, and when the leeks are just starting to brown, add the butter. Pour on top of the chicken. Top with crumbled blue cheese, and pour over the béchamel. If you have made the béchamel in advance, heat it up in a saucepan before pouring it over the chicken and leek mixture. Top with the rolled out piece of puff pastry and cut off any excess. You can allow the pie to cool fully, and then refrigerate, or you can cook it straight away at 180°C (350°F) for 35 minutes. During cooking, the pastry may rise up. If this happens, simply stab it with a knife to let the air out. If you think the pie is getting too golden brown, cover it with tin foil. When the pastry is golden brown and the filling piping hot, it is ready to serve.

White Chocolate Berries

This is a recipe that requires very little organisation. It really is one of the easiest dessert recipes and gives such a great end result – even for non-dessert fans.

300g (10oz) white chocolate
300ml (½ pint) cream
400g (14oz) frozen mixed fruits,
(available in frozen departments in supermarkets)

Preheat your grill to its highest setting.

Break the chocolate into small pieces, and place in a bowl with the cream over a saucepan of gently simmering water. Be careful that the water does not get into the bowl or the chocolate will seize. If this happens, the chocolate will stop melting, and seem to solidify. Just keep on the heat, and add a knob of butter. It will be fine after a few minutes. White chocolate doesn't melt as easily or as quickly as dark chocolate, so it will take about 15 minutes.

Put the frozen berries into a gratin dish. Pour the white chocolate sauce on top. Put under the grill for 5-10 minutes. Serve in tall glasses or individual ramekins.

nchovies Cou

nchovy Egg

lincemeat Fla

pple Crumble

raiche Brulée

ruits, 8 Artich

sparagus Egg

autéed Spina

Roast Vege

Index

it's been fun ...